P9-DFT-641

Love**Knowledge**

8 / '20

LoveKnowledge   Roy Brand

THE LIFE OF
PHILOSOPHY
FROM SOCRATES
TO DERRIDA

Columbia University Press   New York

Columbia University Press
Publishers Since 1893
New York   Chichester, West Sussex
cup.columbia.edu
Copyright © 2013 Columbia University Press
All rights reserved

Library of Congress Cataloging-in-Publication Data
Brand, Roy.
LoveKnowledge: the life of philosophy from Socrates to Derrida/
Roy Brand
p. cm.
Includes bibliographical references (p.) and index.
ISBN 978-0-231-16044-5 (cloth: alk. paper)
—ISBN 978-0-231-16045-2 (pbk.: alk. paper)
—ISBN 978-0-231-53084-2 (e-book)
1. Life. I. Title. II. Title: Love knowledge.

BD431.B7455   2013
190—dc23   2012009205

Columbia University Press books are printed on
permanent and durable acid-free paper. This book
is printed on paper with recycled content.

Printed in the United States of America
c 10 9 8 7 6 5 4 3 2 1
p 10 9 8 7 6 5 4 3 2 1

Cover design by Evan Gafney

References to Internet Web sites (URLs) were accurate
at the time of writing. Neither the author nor Columbia University Press is responsible for Web sites that may
have expired or changed since the book was prepared.

For my parents, Varda and Yoel Brand,
who taught me how to ask without
hesitation and how to answer with
conviction but without certainty.

CONTENTS

PREFACE

All men by nature desire to know.
—Aristotle

This book evolved out of years of engagement with key texts and philosophers in academic journals, conferences, conversations, and classrooms—both as a student and as a professor. At times, the book captures the voice of a student or an interlocutor, and at times—though less often—a professor. In all cases the following pages are the result of close readings or, more concretely, the result of a certain kind of reading—one that emphasizes performance and effect and considers these important vehicles for the philosophical message.

The book's main concern is expressed in its title: *LoveKnowledge*. This, of course, is a distortion of the accepted translation of *philo-sophia* as the "love of knowledge." I should confess at the beginning that the book doesn't offer a rigid, conclusive definition. Instead, the term becomes the question that drives each chapter and is reshaped with each new section. For this is how I myself experienced it. Through long and involved readings, I discovered that my thinking comes back to this fundamental question over and over again, from different perspectives: what is the love that turns into knowledge and how is the knowledge we seek already a form of love? I cannot answer this question, and I cannot explain it away. At best, I follow its different formations in a number of texts, which I consider among the best and most interesting of the philosophical offerings. It is the oldest question of them all; this question gave birth to philosophy two and a half millennia ago and this book does not dare an answer but rather attempts to bring it to life for us today.

Each chapter is a reading of a single book. The texts are idiosyncratic, most of them published after each author's death, and they include reflections on the kind of life philosophy offers, the *life of the mind*—a term that includes a whole spectrum of activities, from doubting to imagining and desiring. My own reading follows the movement of their thinking, the passion that drives the ideas, and the results. The interpretations I provide are at times informed by other writers, and when this is so I mention it clearly in the body of the text rather than in a note. The goal is not to argue directly with other interpretations or to establish a different systematic interpretation. The interest lies elsewhere—in discovering what laces different philosophers together, what motivates them, what they achieve, and why it is important for us today. I do not wish to claim that the readings I present here are complete; at best they provide a glimpse of a philosopher's thought. But the idiosyncratic perspective can also be beneficial. For the professional, it suggests a fresh way to encounter classical texts and form connections between them. For the novice it serves as an opening into the field of philosophy as a form of life, a practice, or an art of existence.

Though this may sound odd in the context of academic philosophy today, the book should also be entertaining. It often renounces didactic explanations and chooses instead to make the richness and ambiguity of each text come to life. It trusts the impressions of the reader and her ability to navigate a philosophical landscape without an outline or map but with a sense of orientation and know-how. Philosophy is, after all, a practice, and to learn it one must be ready to jump in.

LoveKnowledge

UNDOING KNOWLEDGE

Socrates of the *Apology*

The two things to know about Socrates are that he had nothing definitive to say and that he was ugly. Somehow these two features have been transformed in collective lore into the image of wisdom and beauty. Is it so hard to accept that the founding father of philosophy—itself the mother of all the sciences—could be a shabby, unattractive plebeian? Even more interestingly, the transformation of Socrates from mortal rambler to intellectual legend had already begun during his own time. Because he could transform ignorance into a form of wisdom, he could make the unattractive beautiful.

Socrates had nothing to teach, yet is the greatest teacher of them all. How is this possible? The only way to answer this is that the question itself becomes the answer. Socrates is the voice of emptiness, wonder, and doubt that made the philosophical search possible. He is a question mark. Generations of philosophers to come—from Socrates' student Plato to Spinoza, Rousseau, Nietzsche, Foucault, and Derrida, each in his own way—came to inhabit this emptiness. They question, they make us question, live afresh the wonder that is the love of knowledge.

The tradition of unknowingness begins with Socrates. It is a tradition that loves but does not have knowledge, whose love is already knowledge and its knowledge already love. Socrates is the *mouthpiece* or the *mask* through which this love story plays out. A reading of two key texts helps explain why this thinker's legacy still matters to us today, two and a half millennia after its birth.

Introduction to Socrates

Socrates (469–399 BC) is considered the father of philosophy, though he might have preferred a more maternal title. He described himself at times as a midwife who helped others give birth to their own knowledge—a knowledge of themselves. Socrates wasn't the first philosopher, but his predecessors—and the shards of their work that remain—followed mostly religious or poetic traditions. Socrates and his manner of conversing created the philosophic tradition carried on by his student Plato and by Plato's student Aristotle.

Socrates was an Athenian citizen who spent his time in conversations about ethics by asking questions about the good life and the virtues of man. He wrote nothing and claimed that writing is a way of forgetting. Our knowledge of him is restricted to the reports of others: most notably, the dialogues of Plato, the *Memorabilia* of Xenophon, and *The Clouds*, a comic play by Aristophanes. He had a profound impact on many of his contemporaries, and, from a distance of two and a half millennia, his portrait remains fresh and his life almost palpable.

Scholars typically divide his work into the early, middle, and late Platonic dialogues. In each dialogue Socrates is the main speaker, guiding its course through a unique method of questioning. In the early dialogues Socrates focuses primarily on ethical problems (such as what is virtue or what is the good) without ever arriving at a positive conclusion that affirms one view or the other. The middle dialogues mark the development of the student, as Socrates' student Plato seeks answers to the Socratic questions proposed. The late dialogues represent Plato's elaboration, afterthoughts, and even criticism of his own middle period. The first text that concerns us is *The Apology,* from the early period, where Socrates explains his special kind of knowledge. The second, *The Symposium*, comes from the middle period, in which Socrates focuses on his special kind of love. The two together will set the route for us and for philosophy toward the practice of loveknowledge.

An Unapologetic Apology

Plato's *Apology,* one of the most detailed works about Socrates' thinking, tells the story of his public trial: he defended himself against accusations of impiety and irreverence in an irreverent, unapologetic—and some might even say self-indicting—manner. In his testimony Socrates explains that he spends his days in adversarial public conversation with anyone willing to argue with him. He challenges the moral complacency of his fellow citizens and embarrasses them when they cannot answer basic questions such as what is virtue, justice, beauty, or goodness—questions they intuitively think themselves capable of answering. In Plato's portrayal of these early dialogues, Socrates never provides a positive answer to his own questions. Instead he admits that neither he nor anyone else knows the definition of virtue or the good life or anything else that is truly important. His peculiar form of wisdom, as he explains, is the knowledge that he does not know. It is exactly this "negative knowledge" that made the Oracle of Delphi say that he is the wisest of all men.

What is most surprising about the *Apology* as a text is that it is remarkably balanced. Socrates is virtually the only speaker, and he often comes across as arrogant and unsympathetic. One would expect the writer, Plato, to gloss over moments that cause the reader to identify with Socrate's persecutors and instead to admire his teacher's excellence. But what the reader gets is a nuanced portrayal of the living context of philosophy as an activity, not just a static discipline.

What draw us to the figure of Socrates, and what makes this character so alive, is the use of irony. When Socrates speaks eloquently about his inability to speak, or when he knowingly analyzes his lack of knowledge, we feel that the man is not entirely genuine or that his intentions do not match his words. We can sense the tensions between the speaker and what is said, which means that we cannot reduce the speaker to what is spoken. This is remarkable because we are faced with a text, not a person, yet the text brings a person to life, and it does so by showing him becoming other than himself.

In the introduction, Socrates denies that he has any skill in speaking other than the skill of speaking the truth.[1] He asks the judges to excuse his plain speech, which he has been accustomed to using in the marketplace. He also mentions his old age and the fact that he has never been accused before, so he has never appeared in court. His string of excuses amount to a perfect introduction to one of the most brilliant examples of rhetoric, because ironically, after the disclaimers, he delivers a masterpiece of a speech.

His speech conforms perfectly to the rules of rhetoric. The diction is impeccable, and the structure concise. It begins with an introduction, then states his case and outlines the plan of the plea. Then he presents the refutation, a digression, and a summation. This speech shows Socrates to be a master rhetorician. Usually rhetoric is defined as power of persuasion, indifferent to truth. Socrates' speech, on the other hand, aims to discover the truth and excellence of the soul, indifferent to pleasure or pain and irrespective of gratification and personal interests. So the second level of irony is that, in the process of using perfect rhetoric, Socrates proves that rhetoric alone is not enough to win his case. On trial for his life, the man who cannot speak speaks too well—and not well enough.

There is something insolent and arrogant about Socrates' humble claim that he does not know. He seems to be consciously proving the accusation correct while in the process of attempting to refute it. Is his mock-humility a form of suicide by legal means? And what can he mean when he says he knows he does not know? What is it that he knows? Is he sincere in claiming ignorance or is he merely faking it to tempt his interlocutors into conversation?

I believe that Socratic irony does not allow us to decide between these options. His ignorance is both sincere and feigned, or perhaps it is neither. Irony, the famous mark of Socrates, is a force that disturbs the usual binary oppositions. It somehow hovers in between, disturbing or provoking, relating while untying the ends. It is this paradoxical stance—more performance than theory—that makes the lover of knowledge so effective.

Irony is culturally specific. In America today it stands for the reverse of sincerity. The new generation of teenagers excels, so they say, in hiding behind what is called "the mask of irony." They do not let their emotions come forth, and, when they do, these emotions are already distanced from them because they are expressed with an air of self-mockery. Irony can quickly deteriorate into an unproductive sort of detachment. But textual irony functions differently. It allows us to see beyond what is said, which means that it makes us more engaged. We find that our reading of the text and our attitudes toward it are exactly what makes the text meaningful. We, the readers, are part of the dialogue just as much as Socrates' partners in dialogue. Naturally, no text exists without its readers. But this one is more demanding. We are not only reading it, but our impressions and the changes we experience are the very subject of the text. Socrates' slippery speech lulls us into a sense of false confidence that proves, in retrospect, our unknowingness. Here is Socrates. Here is his story. Nothing can be clearer, and we can follow along and evaluate the claims. But then what does he mean? Is he really ignorant, and why would he fake it? This rhetorician who denounces rhetoric proves himself guilty of impiety while arguing against the charge. Now it looks like we are guilty of ignorance and self-delusion. Now we know we don't know; moreover, we realize how natural it is for us to think we know and how difficult and disturbing it might be to discover that we don't. This trial is not Socrates' but ours. This text is not about him but about us. We have no position outside the text, and we too, like Socrates' partners in dialogue, find ourselves unknowingly conversing with a blank mirror. And it proves us ignorant.

The Informal Accusation

Socrates begins his defense by saying that, in addition to his formal plaintiffs, he has a large body of old, informal accusers within Athens. The court of public opinion has already found that he is "a wise man [more like a wise guy], who speculated about the heavens above, and searched into the earth beneath, and made the worse appear the better cause," says Socrates himself (18b). Socrates considers this informal charge more dangerous than the official one. As he says, it is a view that circulates among the Athenians to which he can attach no particular name. His old accusers are the most difficult to deal with, "for it is impossible to bring any one of them forward as a witness and cross-examine him. I must rather, as it were, fight with shadows in making my defense, and question where no one answers" (18d).

In today's terms, fighting with shadows sounds like a metaphor for a struggle with an unconscious opponent. It is of the nature of the unconscious to work in anonymity, like a shadow—a fact that makes the achievement of self-knowledge so difficult. Socrates refers to this old accusation in terms of prejudice. As always, his task is "to remove from you in this short time that prejudice which you have been so long acquiring." He is well aware that his short verbal defense cannot defeat such prejudice but "the law must be obeyed and a defense conducted" (19a).

Socrates is accused of speculating "about the heavens above" and searching "into the earth beneath." What does this accusation by public opinion, which Socrates considers more dangerous than the formal indictment, mean? First we should note that speculating about the heavens above and the earth below does not necessarily mean a physical or metaphysical speculation about the nature of the universe. Aristophanes, the comedian, presented Socrates as such a ridiculous metaphysician, "talking about walking on air and babbling a great deal of other nonsense" (19c). The image of the clumsy, absent-minded, and nonsensical philosopher is already part of the repertoire of comedy in the Greek world. As Socrates is quick to explain, he has no interest in this sort of speculation. But the accusation is serious. Behind the image of the absent-minded philosopher, there is the fear that Socrates' questions disturb the established order of their world—the sky above and the earth bellow. To wit, he questions their general framework for making sense of the world, and therefore his position must seem nonsensical. But, before developing this alternative, we must examine Socrates' own explanation of the fear and hate he arouses.

In order to explain the reasons for the public hostility toward him, Socrates relates the story of the Oracle of Delphi. According to the story, when asked if there was any man wiser than Socrates, the oracle replied that there is none. This response shocked Socrates: "When I heard this I kept thinking: 'what on earth does the god mean? What is he hinting at? For I am aware of not being wise in anything, great or small. What then could he mean by saying that I am wise?'" (21B2–5) The answer seemed itself a paradox, since Socrates knew nothing and yet the god cannot lie. So he embarked upon a mission to solve the riddle and sought out wise men to discover how his knowledge stacked up.

First he went to a politician, who "was thought wise by many, and still wiser by himself" (21c). He soon found that the man was not wise, and Socrates explained this to him. Naturally, the man grew to hate Socrates. Next he went to the poets and asked them to explain the subjects of their eloquent poems, but they were unable to do so. "Then I knew that not by wisdom do the poets write poetry, but by a sort of genius and inspiration" (22c). Then he went to the artisans and found them to be masters of their craft, but ignorant of other subjects. In the process, Socrates says, he made many enemies but found a solution to the oracle's riddle: his wisdom consists in his knowing that he does not know. He concluded that "God only is wise; and by his answer he intends to show that the wisdom of men is worth little or nothing; he is not speaking of

Socrates, he is only using my name by way of illustration, as if he said, he O men, is the wisest, who, like Socrates, knows that his wisdom is in truth worth nothing" (23).

This story helps illustrate the cause for the public hostility toward Socrates, but it is hardly a sufficient explanation for his death. We need something stronger than mere annoyance at an arrogant philosopher in order to understand the fear that Socrates' dialogues agitated. Socrates died a condemned criminal. The accusation of impiety was indeed a serious matter in Athens, because it directly affected the city's welfare and safety. But Socrates was not impious. His manner was perhaps unusual, and his beliefs might have been opaque, but Athens did not persecute men on the basis of their beliefs. In any case, Athenian religion was not a matter of orthodox dogma but a highly developed form of polytheistic folk tradition—ritual and observance—and a general outlook on life supported by myth, not by doctrine.

So why was Socrates charged with among the most serious allegations the Athenian state could claim against a citizen? Why was he condemned and put to death? What matters here are not the specific historical details, but the philosophical importance of his life and death as brought forth in Plato's text. What does this death signify as an event in the history of philosophy?

Questioning World Views

How disturbing Athens must have found Socrates that it would put him to death? There is nothing in the formal accusation that helps us figure this out. And so generations of readers have puzzled over the fact that the first democratic state sentenced its first philosopher to death. But there is more here than mere historic accident. It is precisely the new form of democracy that Socrates disturbs, since democracy relays on consensus, and consensus is based on a common way of experiencing and interpreting the world. Tyranny can tolerate oddity and disagreement so long as it does not influence the state. But a democracy is far less flexible in this respect. It is threatened by the kind of questions he presents. His thinking is radical not because he has different ideas (or because he worships different gods, as the mythic language of the indictment goes) but because he simply questions the existing ones. Impiety means just that—disturbing the unspoken order, that collective unconsciousness that governs the community. As Euthyphro, who is featured as a religious expert in the Platonic dialogue that bears his name, explains: "Piety preserves both families and cities and keeps them safe. The opposite of what is acceptable to the gods is impious, and impiety overturns and destroys all things" (14b). Socrates is a radical cultural critic of sorts. Radical because he has no agenda and defends no dogma but only a few methodic principles that keep the dialogue going. His practice is not impious toward Athenian religion specifically, but toward any belief system, any doctrine, and any order, Athenian or otherwise. Socrates' accusers recognize an important characteristic regarding the Socratic, and indeed the philosophic, way of life.

Much of philosophy has this peculiar character of examining what is most evident and commonplace. It questions the features of life that we take for granted—the views we have grown to accept as givens and realities we take to be natural. Philosophy raises problems we don't usually raise in our everyday life, such as the question regarding the existence of the world or the existence of other minds. We don't raise these questions because, on the whole, we never doubt the existence of the world. We grow accustomed to this order and to a host of other beliefs, which Socrates calls our old prejudices, without examination.

Socrates' practice inserts a measure of uncertainty into our everyday. Some might find this process exciting; others might experience it as endangering deeply rooted ways of life. Socrates' partners in dialogue discover time and again that they cannot justify the most basic features of their existence or that their existence is based on a set of assumptions they leave unexamined. His interrogation leaves them unhinged. Some find relief and freedom in being loosed from this foundation, but many become anxious and fearful. The Socratic practice is meant to tap into the former and make us accept our lack of knowledge as a source of liberation, joy, and motivation to continue seeking greater understanding.

The Socratic *Elenchus*

The Socratic investigation asks us to formulate explicitly the views that shape who we are. Usually, those beliefs are too close to be noticed. We are blind to the overall picture that defines our identities, since it stands at the background of our world, providing an invisible framework through which all of our experiences are channeled.

So we can already suggest an answer to the general questions: what kind of knowledge is Socrates aiming for, by what means, and for what end? The knowledge his questions intend to probe is the knowledge of *ourselves*—the knowledge of who we are, what beliefs we hold, and what convictions shape the way we experience our world. The process helps shape a life of continuous self-examination in which every conviction is brought up to face the scrutiny of reason. Living a life of self-examination does not mean a constant judging of oneself, but a practice of elaborating on what one is. But we still have to answer the question regarding the means for achieving the examined life. How does Socrates get us to question the underlying suppositions that inform our daily lives even when we aren't entirely aware of them?

The Socratic method is a form of a critical investigation called *elenchus* (ἔλεγχος), which literally means "to examine critically" or "to censure." In fact, the philosophy of Socrates consists in nothing more and nothing less than this method of investigation. It relies on the premise that Socrates, following his disavowal of knowledge, avoids asserting nearly any positive content. The most precise description of the Socratic elenchus was given by Gregory Vlastos, an authority on classic philosophy and Socrates in particular: "Socratic elenchus is a search for moral truth by question-and-answer adversary argument in which a thesis is debated only if asserted as the answerer's own belief and is regarded as refuted only if its negation is deduced from his own beliefs."[2] It is important that the elenchus is a search for moral rather than abstract, practical, or objective truth. The Socratic method is oriented toward the good life or happiness. This is intimately related to morality since, for the Greeks, it is impossible to enjoy happiness while being immoral. The good, the beautiful, the true, and the wise are all connected; hence it is only by virtue of having a good character that one can achieve the good life. The person who is practicing self-perfection, who cares for himself, is also the person whose actions are best for others and for the state. The Socratic demand to "know thyself" is simultaneously a demand for self-examination and for moral consciousness.

The search for moral truth necessitates the "question-and-answer adversary argument." It is only the course of the conversation and not the abstract logic of the argument that can lead the participants to such truth. Finding philosophy through dialogue seems at first like an unusual way to go about the discipline. The dialogic tradition borrows heavily from fiction, and especially from drama, a form that was perfected before Socrates' methodical examination. But here it serves as a vehicle not for storytelling but for finding truth. So, on a deeper level, the emphasis on dialogue represents a different conception of knowledge in which intelligence is not held by one person as a possession. Instead, it becomes a process between at least two interlocutors. Knowledge is relational or dialectical. It requires a double, and the meaning of the knowledge gained in the process is always circumscribed by the context of the exchange.

This different conception of knowledge goes hand in hand with a different conception of self. An individual is not an object-like thing that can be examined in isolation, but rather a temporal creation that unfolds by means of a dialogic process. Contrary to present-day prophets of self-discovery, there is no way to stop and take hold of ourselves. Simply put, there is no authentic core you discover when you probe yourself. Rather, knowing oneself requires a commitment to travel outside of oneself and join with others. Self-knowledge is a destination not an origin. At the beginning, before examination, we are strangers to ourselves.

But in another respect authenticity is an important part of the Socratic method. "Say what you believe" is the only condition for entering into a debate. A person whose statements express his beliefs endows his words with the significance of his own life. One does not simply assert a hypothesis, but arguments proceed on the basis of the participants' beliefs. That means that investigations of these hypotheses become an *existential self-examination*. Any move in the debate will have an effect on one's set of beliefs and hence on the way one understands oneself.

In this sense Socrates foreshadows the way modern thinkers emphasize embodied knowledge. Words can be used to imagine or describe, to mount hypothesis or to theorize, but Socrates wants speech to have the effect of a performative promise. It essentially amounts to the claim: here I am, here is what I believe in, here is myself. Anything less will be mere gesturing in the air.

The demand for "truthful expression" seems to conflict with the ironic style so characteristic of Socrates. But, as we have seen, irony does not mean saying something and meaning something else. Socratic irony is a feature of the text, which allows us to detect a life that cannot be captured in words. It is this ambiguity and essential vacillation that amount to Socratic irony. Yes, there is a distance between what one says and what one is, but that distance is a motivating force that propels the investigation forward.

Irony today might at bottom say that "I don't really mean what I'm saying." As a cultural norm it might even amount to the claim that it is impossible to mean what you say. How different this is from Socratic irony, which urges us to mean exactly what we say and admit that closing the gap between what we are and what we express is impossible. As we shall see following a reading of the *Symposium*, it is in this gap that love finds its place, as love takes up where knowledge leaves off.

Socrates as a Protopsychoanalyst

The similarities between the Socratic method of elenchus and the psychoanalytic technique have been noted by many commentators.[3] This is no accident, as Freud was an admirer of the classical period and referred to the author of the Socratic texts as "the divine Plato."[4]

First, the Socratic method of cross-examination is designed to bring out beliefs that underlie the respondent's claims, about which he might even be unaware himself. In this sense Socrates is engaged in an effort to enlarge the realm of consciousness at the expense of the unconscious.

But it is important to note that the Socratic unconscious is far from a vulgar conception of the unconscious as a storehouse of repressed thoughts or desires—though this understanding of unconscious is an oversimplification of Freud's original theory. To both thinkers the unconscious—or the part of oneself that represents "not knowing"—is what shapes and channels what we know, believe, think, and experience. The unconscious is not a repository of repressed thoughts and desires but a dynamic process of selection: it ascribes value and determines context and relation. In short, the *not* of knowledge or the *un* of consciousness are inherently active in determining what we know or what we are conscious of.

Second, Socrates' single condition that a person says what she believes bares a remarkable resemblance to the fundamental psychoanalytic principle that requires the patient to state whatever comes into her mind without censorship. The point of both principles of analysis is to reveal that person's set of psychic commitments because only if one is committed to what one says will the process of questioning have any real effect on the self.

It's important not to conflate the two traditions, however. As compared to the Socratic tradition, psychoanalysis claims a broader jurisdiction over psychic commitments. It goes beyond the "not knowing" to include behavioral and involuntary evidence such as unconscious slips, free associations, dreams, and other acts that manifest the working of the psyche.

Third, both Socrates and Freud believed in the power of the spoken word to elicit change in attitudes and character. Socrates perfected the technique of an asymmetrical dialogue, in which the one side—the side Freud would call the analyst's—serves as an empty screen on which the fantasies, desires, traumas, and frustrations of the patient are projected and then confronted consciously and deliberately. Socrates describes himself as a midwife, helping his partner become aware of himself and in this way achieve virtue and happiness. The marked difference between the two traditions is that Socrates also worked on himself. He rejected any fixed position and shaped himself instead as the philosopher while helping others know or become themselves. This positions him closer to a partner in dialogue, with equal responsibilities and privileges.

Finally, the Socratic question of how one should live (which is, in every case, personal, i.e., how *I* should live) is the only fundamental question of psychoanalysis. It provides both the means and the end of psychoanalytic therapy. Socrates understood that people become who they are in the process of asking and answering this question. And the process of making this question explicit allows us to rethink and recreate ourselves according to our own principles That is why, for Socrates, the unexamined life is not worth living, and confronting this problem requires examining how and why the question is lost in everyday routines. How does life become something we take for granted? And, more important, how we can bring it up to awareness again? The Socratic method, like psychoanalysis, opens a space for self-examination. It does not provide answers since the question itself—how I should live—is already the way toward virtue and happiness.

Both the analytical setting and Socrates' elenchus function dialogically, but the power dynamics is different in each case. In analysis, we begin by thinking that the psychoanalyst knows something more than we do. After all, the treatment means paying a certified professional who has undergone years of training. Participating in therapy involves trusting that an analyst will see through our self-distortions, recognizes our veils, and decipher our inner self—or that's what we want to believe. But, as therapy progresses, we often learn that the analyst knows very little about us. She only knows what we tell her and what we care to reveal through our behavior, stories, thoughts, and dreams. As analysis progresses, we learn to use the practice differently. The analyst becomes a mirror through which we learn about ourselves. The mirror knows nothing. Instead, it simply delivers us back to ourselves.

Socrates' power dynamics work in the reverse way. The conversation partner begins thinking he knows better than this arrogant and disheveled old man. Though Socrates already has a reputation for his relentless questioning, the conversation partner thinks he can outsmart Socrates: "maybe others have fallen into his traps, but I fully understand the principles by which I live my life." This statement, which makes the "I" an exception, is shared by the reader as well. The only difference is that the reader thinks she can outsmart both Socrates and his interlocutors, by seeing how they are led, unknowingly, to the position of not knowing. But, as the dialogue progresses, the roles gradually reverse. The reader observes Socrates as he outsmarts his accusers. But then we are dumbfounded as readers, since outsmarting the accusers, by showing his skill to unsettle conviction, only hastens Socrates' conviction and death. The reader loses her self-confidence. Is Socrates a wise man feigning ignorance, or is he a fool pretending to be a wise man? The irony soon hits the reader on the head: the teacher proves himself at once powerful and impotent. And this is precisely the lesson. No one can tell us how to live our lives. But, without an incitement, we forget to ask it ourselves. We need to be fooled by a wise guy to appreciate the significance of the forgotten question.

The Irony of Irony

How are we to make sense of Socrates' disavowal of knowledge? Is he sincere in claiming not to know and asking others for answers, or is he deceitful in pretending not to know in order to lure others into conversation? What does it mean to know that you don't know?

Otto Apelt, a German philosopher and editor of Plato's work, has described the Socratic technique as a process of splitting and doubling (*spaltung und verdoppelung*).[5] Apelt describes Socrates as filling two roles simultaneously: the one who knows and the one who does not. This division creates a tension in the reading: as we try to figure out if Socrates is sincere in claiming ignorance, we are split as readers as well—switching positions between knowing and not knowing.

In other words, irony isn't just a rhetorical device for Socrates. It's an essential part of unsettling the reader to make him internalize the questions he poses. Socrates' irony is not an instrument in the service of ideas but, as the famous existential philosopher Søren Kierkegaard says, it is his position itself: "Socrates' life is like a magnificent pause in the course of history: we do not hear him at all; a profound stillness prevails—until it is broken by the noisy attempt of the many different schools of followers to trace their origin in this hidden and cryptic source. His irony was not the instrument he used in the service of the idea; irony was his position—more he did not have."[6] Kierkegaard defines irony as "infinite absolute negativity." Irony is the voice of negativity itself. This is the doubling effect of irony. It splits the actual moment in two and makes one face the other. But the act of splitting itself is completely empty. It is simply the first, purely abstract move in helping us realize our capacity to reflect, by confronting us with ourselves and opening up the space for self-examination.

The internal split within Socrates is doubled in the reader. The reader too splits and doubles in the process of reading or conversing with the text. The effect is that of self-transformation—becoming other than oneself. This effect was unknown to the

Athenians of Socrates' time, and it is the source of the charges of impiety and corruption against him (24). He is guilty of being the first individual of the Athenian democracy—the first to stand independently of the conventions and customs of his age. Moreover, he is guilty of teaching others how to develop this individuality and therefore guilty of corrupting others who can now stand on their own as well. The accusations against him—both formal and informal—are entirely correct. Socrates is guilty because of his technique. Both simple and elusive, his technique is irony. Socrates is an empty persona—a mask through which we learn to speak for ourselves. He is our demon or our gadfly (30–31), and his questions amount to an invocation to examine our lives. As he professes at the end of his unapologetic defense, he knows nothing but to teach how to "care for the self."

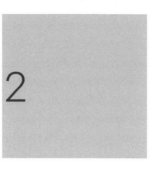

THE LOGIC OF DESIRE

Socrates of the *Symposium*

Philosophy is not just about knowledge but also about love. There is no love without knowledge and no knowledge without love. Love without knowledge becomes more like an animal drive, and knowledge without love is reduced to a simple search for information. The two are necessary, but they do not form a harmonious couple. Their struggle, which we here call loveknowledge, defines us as humans and their particular configuration in each of us makes us who we are.

In the last chapter we saw how Socrates became the embodiment of knowledge that knows its limitations. In questioning his accusers, he caused others to reflect on their own lives and made the reader engage with the story not just as an outside observer but as an active participant. But how did he live these questions himself? What form did his love take, and how did it come to inhabit the space the knowledge leaves out?

In the *Symposium* we see Socrates as a primary actor engaged in a performance of love, desire, and knowledge. This performance represents a new genre, one that grows out of the ~~already~~ existent, honored tradition of tragedy, but adds irony and comedy. Socrates becomes a new type of hero—classical in the trial he experiences, but modern in that he is sacrificed not by fate but by his own conscious confrontation with emptiness.

The Socratic tragicomedy brings forth a hero who preaches no message and who resists deification. It is a parody of tragedy since the hero does not wish to ascend beyond human knowledge, but rather stays strictly within its limitations. The irony is that this very faithfulness to being human transgresses the boundaries of social acceptance, as if being entirely what one is, being just that— an individual—is inconceivable and disturbing.

As French philosopher Pierre Hadot explains: "An immense desire arises from such an awareness of privations and this is why, for Western consciousness, Socrates the philosopher takes on the features of Eros, the eternal vagabond in search of true ~~beauty~~."[1] Socrates, the man who knows his limitations, is also the embodiment of *eros*.

Introduction to the *Symposium*

One of the most beautiful features of the *Symposium* is that it renders the life of philosophy concrete and visible. It is an account of a banquet given by the young and beautiful poet Agathon on the occasion of his victory at the dramatic contest in Athens—the equivalent of an Academy Award—in 416 BC. A number of male friends gather together to drink and offer their praises. Socrates, over fifty at the time, is by far the oldest participant. His presence partly explains why the female flautist, who provides both musical and sexual entertainment, is sent away and the participants decide to offer their praises to eros.

As in the case of the *Apology*, the reader is literally drawn into the storyline. We can hear the speakers gather in a house surrounded by golden fields of wheat, dotted by olive trees, and sprinkled with low grapevines in between. We can hear the clinking of the glasses, the maidservant coming in with jars of wine and "small-plates" to allow the drinking to go on.

Eros—the subject of all speeches—can be translated as both love and desire. The general Greek word for love is *philia*, which applies generally to a person's feelings for family, friends, and lovers. *Eros*–the word used in the *Symposium*—refers more to an intense desire or attachment and covers the entire spectrum of passion, from sexual lust to otherworldly contemplation. The versatility of the Greek's term caused Freud to choose it in constructing his theory of sexuality. As he explains, it mediates the tension between the rational and the animal, the abstract and the lustful: "In its origin, function and relation to sexual love, the *eros* of the philosopher Plato coincides exactly with the love-force, the libido of psychoanalysis."[2] And again, "what psychoanalysis calls sexuality was by no means identical with the impulsion towards a union of the two sexes or towards producing a pleasurable sensation in the genitals; it had far more resemblance to the all-inclusive and all-embracing love of Plato's *Symposium*."[3]

To begin with, love—as it is described in the *Symposium*—is primarily homosexual love, and the praises offered to the god of love are reflected, projected, or transferred onto the relations between the men at the banquet. The term *sym-posium* literally means "drinking-together"—though of course the Greeks considered it uncivilized to drink without engaging in conversation, songs, and celebration for the gods. After concluding a round of discussion in which each participant delivered a small speech in praise of eros, Alcibiades, a well-known beauty, suddenly appears. He is the former lover of Socrates and the present lover of Agathon. After entering drunkenly, Alcibiades quarrels with Socrates and the former lovers show their rivalry over Agathon. This petty lovers' spat both accentuates and contrasts the tragicomic speeches given by each participant.

The Myth of Aristophanes

The guests offer their speeches in order from left to right, making Socrates, who come to the feast late and shares Agathon's couch, the last to speak. The first three speeches are rather conventional, though they reveal Athenian society's hypocrisy with respect to male love and especially the love between men and boys. Aristophanes, who is known as the father of comedy, heats up the discussion. This is the same Aristophanes whose play *The Clouds* is mentioned in the *Apology* as the source of the common misconception of philosophy as an idle ramble. Plato, who wrote this a generation or so after the events, makes Aristophanes tell a myth explaining the origin and nature of the force that drives humans toward each other. As the myth goes, human beings were originally created in three sexes: male, female, and a combination of the two—androgynous. These protohumans had twice as many organs as we do today and they had great strength. This strength brought about their demise, since their hubris was so great that they attempted to ascend to heaven and attack the gods. As a punishment, Zeus split them in half. As Aristophanes explains, "Love is born into every human being; it calls back the halves of our original nature together; it tries to make one out of two and heal the wound of human nature."[4] Love is the desire to find our other original half, and our sexual preferences are determined by the sex of our double. Aristophanes' myth thus explains both homosexual and heterosexual love as natural, even biologically determined.

There are several points that follow from this stunning account. First, it resembles the myth of the Tower of Babel, which tells the story of our ancestors' attempt to ascent to heaven, to become like the gods. Both these legends result in a fall and a subsequent splitting, though in the Tower of Babel it is not our bodies but our tongues that are split into hundreds of incompatible languages. Second, this story anticipates a modern conception that describes love as a force drawing two individuals together to form a unified whole. Third, it is highly pessimistic because a final or absolute reunion of our halves is impossible. The physical union of two to form one is possible only as a fleeting moment of sexual intercourse, so the goal of loving can never be achieved in a sustained way. Humans are left with the desire to reunite with their other halves and the repeated frustration of their persistent, obsessive attempts to complete this reunion.

Our desire for another is testimony to our inherent lacking and our incompleteness. In Plato's telling of the evening, Aristophanes says, "we used to be complete wholes in our original nature, and now 'Love' is the name for our pursuit of wholeness, for our desire to be complete" (192E). Desire is intended to restore an original state before the splitting into halves. It is born out of lack and sustains itself because of this lack. When this drive is allowed to run loose, it develops a fixation on an imaginary "original" state of union and bliss such as the desire to unite with the mother or to return to a state prior to language or culture. But such a desire, to unite with the mother or to live outside culture or language, is at the same time the death of the desiring subject.

Socrates is not alone in his conception of desire as arising from a need for completion. Other thinkers such as French psychoanalyst, Jacque Lacan, described human desire as "the desire of the Other."[5] Likewise, G. W. F. Hegel, in his classic theory of dialectics, described the relationship between mastery and servitude as turning desire not simply toward the body or an individual, but toward the *desire* of another person.

One desires the desire of another—even a child knows and experiences this. One naturally desires to be desired by the other. But the stability of such a system is always at risk since it is always alive and open: I cannot posses the desire of another and the other cannot posses mine. The offering of desire must be mutual, circular, and self-supporting: I desire your desire desiring my desire and so on.

Of course, this very circularity is often experienced not as love but as misery and dissatisfaction. One possible solution is to reject desire altogether and to substitute the desire of the other. In other words, I can accommodate myself to another's desire by choosing the same target and craving it in the same manner. Both parties might find this pleasurable at first. The individual who has given up his independent desires can now live without their complica tions, and the other has her wish fulfilled completely by her partner. But both people will eventually become unsatisfied. Since the relinquisher is dead to his own desires, he lives without pain but also without pleasure. Meanwhile, the desirer doesn't get what she wants—the other's desire—but a facsimile of her own desire.

An alternative scenario (and happier, at least to my mind—but who can judge between pleasures?) takes place when both parties acknowledge their inherent deficiencies and work within this framework. Acknowledging our incompleteness is a recognition of a certain tension necessary for our constitution and life.

From this perspective, Socrates' acknowledgment of his ignorance and his unwillingness to accept an overly simplified solution is an outstanding achievement. His process shows us how to move away from a sense of false completion and toward eros, a living and mutually reinforcing desire that perpetuates itself. Eros, as Socrates understands it, is desire made progressive. It still yearns to achieve union, but it finds stability not by regressing to an impossible, Eden-like state prior to the split, but by accepting the vicissitudes of life and altering itself accordingly. Stability is achieved through change, by constantly becoming different and recreating oneself. That is the tall mark of a Socratic pursuit of knowledge. But this conception is not handed down to us from above, as if a moral or a theory has been conveyed. The text literally carries us forward, from one speech to the next, to appreciate and evaluate different understandings of desire that affect and shape who we are and how we live. Soon Socrates' own story is revealed by way of enactment rather than a direct story line. It is a story of sublimation through self-mastery, though not without its pleasures.

Socrates Questions Agathon

In many ways Socrates' speech, which comes last but is then followed by the unexpected entrance of his former young lover, Alcibiades, complements the views Aristophanes expresses. The only major difference is that Socrates describes the split of halves in philosophic rather than mythological terms. His claims are based on the principle we just derived—that one desires what one lacks. Since eros is the desire for beauty, and one cannot desire what one already has or is, eros cannot itself be beautiful. By this point in the dialogue, eros is not merely a Greek god but, like all Greek gods, a distilled representation of human passions. We should note that for the ancient Greeks the beautiful is also the good. Since all good things are beautiful, eros cannot be good or virtuous either.

As Agathon finishes his speech, he praises eros as the youngest, most beautiful, and most virtuous of all the gods. "Love was born to hate old age and will come nowhere near it. Love always lives with young people and is one of them: the old story holds good that like is always drawn to like," he says (195B). This is meant only partly as a critique of Socrates, the oldest and least beautiful of the group. But Socrates follows with a counterassertion, claiming that eros is neither young nor beautiful nor virtuous. If this were simply a charge leveled against a god, it would be both reckless and irreverent. But Socrates circumscribes his words and makes clear that eros is neither a god nor human but a movement that travels between what one is and what one is not, similar to the experience of desire. Having silenced Agathon, Socrates regains his position both in the explicit game of celebrating eros and in the implicit game of praising oneself. As always, his claims are a mix of arrogance and humility.

Next, he tells the story of Diotima—a mysterious priestess he met when he was young and his teacher in matters of love. This is perhaps the first and certainly one of the rare occasions that a woman appears in a philosophical text. It is unique also because she does not appear in person but rather through Socrates' reenactment of her as a teacher who taught him, when he was younger, the art of love. Diotima is then the teacher of the first teacher of philosophy.

Diotima's Account: Eros Falls Between the Human and the Divine

Agathon's mistake lies in conceiving of eros as a model of the beloved and as inherently beautiful, virtuous, and young. Diotima suggests an alternative in which eros is more like the lover than like the beloved. As lover, eros desires beauty, virtue, and youth, but is not necessarily young, virtuous, or beautiful himself (204A). That's not to say that Diotima envisions eros as ugly or bad—it's simply that eros exists outside the logic of binary dichotomies. It is neither beautiful nor ugly, neither good nor bad. Eros is the movement between the poles; it never attains beauty or the good, but it always progresses toward them. The careful reader can already hear the resonance of Socrates' own movement toward knowledge, which he never has but always desires. As Socrates relates her story, the connection between eros and his own occupation soon becomes explicit by equating the logic of desire with knowledge:

> DIOTIMA: "Watch your tongue! Do you really think that if a thing is not beautiful, it has to be ugly?"
>
> SOCRATES: "I certainly do."
>
> DIOTIMA: "And if a thing is not wise, it's ignorant? Or haven't you found out yet that there's something in between wisdom and ignorance?"
>
> SOCRATES: "What's that?"
>
> DIOTIMA: "It's judging things correctly without being able to give a reason. Surely you see this is not the same as knowing—for how could knowledge be unreasoning? And it's not ignorance either—for how could what hits the truth be ignorance? Correct judgment, of course, has this character it is *in between* understanding and ignorance" (201E–202A).

Eros, as Diotima explains, is not strictly a god, nor is he mortal either. According to Diotima, "He's a great spirit. Everything spiritual, you see, is in between god and mortal" (202D-E). Diotima equates beauty and wisdom by describing eros as a lover and pursuer of virtue instead of as a beloved or possessor of virtues. This explanation makes clear that the pursuit of wisdom is motivated by love—in fact, it is love's highest expression.

Love and Immortality

We already saw that love can never completely possess its target. When the object of desire is achieved, desire dies out. What, then, is the point of loving when love is doomed to failure? What is the point of loving knowledge when we already know we cannot have it? As Socrates asks Diotima: "All right then, my friend. What you say about Love is beautiful, but if you're right, what use is Love to human beings?" (204C–D)

The attempt to answer this question leads to dialectical spirals that have confounded even the greatest thinkers. Diotima defines eros as the desire for happiness, which she and Socrates interpret as an attempt to possess the good forever (204E–205A). But since humans are not immortal, they cannot posses the good forever, thus they cannot achieve lasting happiness. Eros resolves that conflict through reproduction—if we cannot be here forever, at least we can leave behind a legacy in our offspring or through our ideas. Eros is therefore the human way of achieving immortality. As Diotima says, eros is the desire to reproduce and to "give birth in beauty, whether in body or in soul" (206B, E).

We should note that this conception of desire accepts and embraces its human limitations. It is a process of education, like the one Socrates undergoes with Diotima. Desire wants immortality but cannot have it, so it shapes itself accordingly and finds resolution in birth, either of body or mind. The education we require is not how to become more like the gods but how to live, simply and entirely, as humans.

Philosophy—at least the kind Socrates practiced—establishes an erotic desire with respect to oneself. Self-knowledge is the knowledge of one's limitation, and to know one's limitation is to transcend one's former self. Mortals achieve immortality not by remaining static but by constantly overcoming and reshaping their former selves. As Diotima explains to the young Socrates: "In that way everything mortal is preserved, not, like the divine, by always being the same in every way, but because what is departing and aging leaves behind something new, something such that it had been. By this device, Socrates, she said, what is mortal shares in immortality, whether it is a body or anything else, while the immortal has another way" (208A–B).

✓ The Theory of Ideas

The search for immortality can never be separated from the search for humanity; in fact these are two sides of the same coin. Diotima attempts to explain this seeming paradox as she says, "the immortal has another way." Her explanation, usually known as Plato's Theory of Ideas, describes the progression of eros from the love of a beautiful body to the love of all beautiful bodies to the love of beauty in the sciences, in law, and finally to the love of Beauty itself (211B–C).

When love attains this highest level, desire finds a resting place in contemplating the abstract concept of beauty itself. This state is stable because love no longer seeks out a fleeting thing in life, but a pure idea of the mind. This conclusion sounds like the cliché wherein philosophy is an abstract and simply theoretical discipline that ignores the things we see and touch in favor of theoretical constructions understood by the mind's eye. But Diotima's view of erotic desire refutes this misconception of philosophy. She

empir

explains immortality as a form of impregnation in body or mind. It is part of the traveling nature of eros that it is both very flashlike and abstract, both body and mind.

So Diotima's speech shows two ways that the desire for immortality can take shape: either it can become an erotic force of reproduction (in body or mind) or it can become fixated on the eternal. The point of the dialogue is not to choose between these two options, but to understand the circuitous path of desire. We are the creatures that will forever experience desire as moving in between reproduction and change, on the one hand, and everlasting presence, on the other. We cannot do with either the one *or* the other, though both together are impossible.

This paradox is implicit in the pursuit and love of knowledge. In the previous chapter we interpreted knowledge as a search that turns on itself to discover its limitation. Here desire undergoes a similar process of self-reflection and self-limitation. From both ends loveknowledge returns to the condition of being human. Knowledge must always be limited and know its limit; likewise love must include its own inner limit so that it can be sustained. Love is not something to know, but something to live by and act. Love demands love, not knowledge, as a response. It cannot be explained, but only performed. This is the performance played out in the *Symposium,* and it is brought to its drunken climax with the entrance of Alcibiades.

The Tragicomic Nature of Philosophy

Acting out the duality of loveknowledge takes shape as both a tragedy and a comedy. It is tragic because it ends in failure and it is comic because it *repeatedly* ends in failure. Socrates becomes the personification of this ironic tragicomedy, and, stylistically, the text underscores the combination of genres. It alternates between a serious philosophical treatise and a drunken ramble. Alcibiades' entrance represents one notch closer to lighthearted debauchery. After he arrives, Alcibiades is asked to make his own contribution in praise of eros. He refuses because he says that Socrates is too jealous to tolerate praise for another, even a god, in his presence. What follows is what philosopher Jonathan Lear calls a "bitchy squabble" over who is jealous of whom.[6] By the end, the participants permit Alcibiades to praise Socrates instead of eros. Given the connection between eros, the lover of beauty and good, and Socrates, the lover of knowledge, this shift does not amount to a change of subject but rather to a more clear presentation of it.[7]

Alcibiades' speech is a mocking tribute to Socrates and emphasizes the ironic, deceitful, double character of his ex-lover. He begins by describing Socrates as the statue of Silenus—the semi-divine companion of Dionysus. Silenus is far from beautiful on the outside, but he contains beautiful little figures of the gods inside. Again Socrates represents not physical beauty, but a vessel containing beautiful ideas. His desire is to impregnate not in body but in mind. Alcibiades is shocked to discover that he, an attractive young man, found himself pursuing the old rag: "as if I were his lover and he my young prey!" (217C). And so Alcibiades concludes his diatribe: "He has deceived us all: he presents himself as your lover, and before you know it, you're in love with him yourself!" (222B).

For Alcibiades, everything is part of the drama of possession and rejection. He is therefore unable to appreciate Socrates' attempt to initiate him to a more "Platonic" conception of love, which cannot be consummated in a one-night stand. Socrates is deceitful, according to Alcibiades, because he turns from the lover to the beloved. Socrates is unattractive on the outside but full of beauty within. Given his looks and his old age, he cannot expect to be pursued by a beautiful young boy, but that is what happened in the course of their relationship—the lover turned into the beloved. Alcibiades does not seem to appreciate the irony he describes. Socrates is doubled, both lover and beloved, having and not having the virtues desired.

This portrayal of Socrates resembles the original man in Aristophanes' myth. Complete unto himself, he possesses his other half and is therefore divine. But the comic and even ridiculous character of Alcibiades shows a common misunderstanding of Socrates. Socrates' double nature does not mean that the two sides are ultimately reconciled in perfect harmony. Instead, the two sides exist in perpetual tension, which is why he remains an erotic figure. His nature is to tempt and resist and to sustain and overcome itself. His knowledge does not remain peacefully within himself, but instead it comes alive in the company of others to provoke, agitate, and challenge them. He is pregnant and therefore he needs partners in dialogue with which to "give birth in beauty, whether in body or in soul" (206B, E).

At the end of their erotic journey toward their other halves, most of the dinner guests have gone home or fallen asleep. Socrates talks to the two who remain: Aristophanes, the famous writer of comedies, and Agathon, the honored tragic poet. The details of their discussion are lost on another drunk and tired onlooker who, in Plato's retelling, "couldn't remember exactly what they were saying . . . but the main point was that Socrates was trying to prove to them that authors should be able to write both comedy and tragedy: the skillful tragic dramatist should also be a comic poet" (223D). Even in style, philosophy is ironic—it moves in between, it is neither the one nor the other. Socrates is the first hero of a new genre. The rest of the thinkers we read here form part of the tradition of loveknowledge as they lend their unique voices to this mask.

3

UNDER A CERTAIN FORM OF ETERNITY

Spinoza's *Ethics*

Baruch de Spinoza (1632–1677), a philosopher who preferred to grind and polish lenses rather than to lecture in the university, confronted the distorted beliefs of his time and sought to correct them by means of a fine-tuned geometric form of writing. His master work, the *Ethics*, published posthumously, proves beyond all doubt that we can achieve a blessed state of happiness by a peculiar mix he calls "intellectual love," and this state can be achieved without institutional religion or any other ritual or magic.

Spinoza is the great champion of concrete life in modern times. It is interesting that philosophy, religion, myth, and ideology often focus on denying the simple facts of life by inventing alternative stories—predicated on the fear of death—that grip our imagination and occupy our mind. Like Socrates, Spinoza diverges from this tradition and constructs his philosophy around the notion that "a free man thinks of nothing less than of death, and his wisdom is a meditation on life, not on death."[1] Spinoza's main interest is to make life noticeable in its natural, simple everydayness. In Spinoza's work, life is no longer a mysterious stream, a divine gift, or an essence, but the concrete web of connections in which we are always immersed. In part the leveling of all forms of existence to a common plane explains why Spinoza is relevant to contemporary thought and practices, from biology to philosophy and art. In part, this equalizing, which denies external moral judgment and pre-established hierarchies, is still difficult for most of us to accept.

The *Ethics* partakes in the age-old task of philosophy—raising the question of how we live and bringing the shape of our life to consciousness. Its emphasis on life as it happens places the *Ethics* on a collision course with monotheistic religions, whose narratives depend on a transcendent divine force. While in modern times transcendent religion has lost its gripping power, Spinoza's ideas are still radical because he denies that individual subjects can know otherworldly truths or act freely outside the chain of necessity. We might find parts of his view appealing and parts appalling, but the argument stems from his uncompromising emphasis on this life and this world and nothing beyond.

Spinoza's work is an anomaly. Even today readers confront it with a mixture of reverence and fear, as his pronouncements strike us as both alien and clear. He invented his own style of writing that mimicked the form of Euclidian geometry. He begins by offering a set of definitions and axioms, moves on to propositions and explanations, and ends with the triumphant QED associated with traditional Euclidian proofs.

In his personal life he challenged some of the most cherished beliefs of his times and ours. He rejected the appeal to an external source of value, and with that he refuted the duality of the material and the spiritual, the eternal and the temporal, the necessary and the contingent. For more than a century after his death, his name was synonymous with atheism and wickedness. He published two books in his lifetime—the first, on the philosophy of René Descartes, did not include his own beliefs. And the second, on matters of theology and politics, was published anonymously and under the name of a false publisher. The *Ethics*, undoubtedly his masterwork, was brought to print only after his death. Inasmuch as it was and still is influential, it is also an eccentric book that does not sit neatly within the traditional history of philosophy. On the one hand, it returns to the ancient tradition of doing philosophy as a practice and a way of life and, on the other, it does so with a modern vocabulary borrowed from the new science and philosophy of the time.

Spinoza's Secret Life and Texts

Eighteen years after the death of his mother and two years after the death of his father, Baruch d'Espinoza, then twenty-eight, was banished from the Jewish community of Amsterdam. The city's relatively new and still fragile collection of immigrants consisted mostly of Spanish and Portuguese Jews who were forced to convert to Christianity at the time of the Spanish Inquisition in 1492. Their persecution, nevertheless, persisted. For more than a century, the converted were harshly interrogated about the depth and sincerity of their beliefs. Spinoza's parents had been such Marrano Christians—the term for Jews who had to live under false pretense as Christians. When the city council of Amsterdam offered citizenship to "Portuguese merchants" in 1598, thousands of crypto-Jews left for the city where they could openly practice a religion they only vaguely remembered.

Many readers of Spinoza link his radically free and independent spirit to his experience with the pretense and irrationality associated with organized religions. His philosophy can be read as a persistent attempt to tear down the veil of myth, irrational fear, and messianic hope that sustains prejudice. Spinoza embraces the world as it is—a world free from higher purposes or an observing, judging God. It is a vision that is as radical as it is simple.

Spinoza's Amsterdam was one of the most liberal cities of Europe, the financial capital of a vibrant new republic enjoying its first golden age. In the year of his birth the great painter Johannes Vermeer and the scientist Antoni van Leeuwenhoek, who developed the microscope, were born in Delft. Spinoza came from a family of traders who used their network of connections across the Iberian peninsula and North Africa to exchange goods. They kept a house alongside a prosperous canal in what was gradually becoming the Jewish quarter. In 1639, when Spinoza was seven, Rembrandt bought a house across the street after marrying the niece of his art dealer who lived next door.

The young Spinoza was well educated in religion and commerce, spoke Portuguese, Spanish, Dutch, and Latin, and received training from non-Jewish teachers in science, philosophy, politics, and classical literature. It is unclear when his religious doubts began, but from his own account in the (unfinished) *Treatise on the Emendation of the Intellect* we know that he found no solace or happiness in the life of a well to do merchant. Gradually, he distanced himself from the Jewish community and focused increasingly on the new philosophy of Descartes as well as on physics, optics, and geometry.

The leaders of the Jewish community in Amsterdam were concerned about his circle of secular acquaintances and rumored atheistic beliefs and asked him to repent. When he refused, they issued a harsh statement of condemnation that amounted to an excommunication. Spinoza's life in Amsterdam became very difficult after this pronouncement. A fanatic reportedly tried to kill him, and he was cut off from his family and source of income. He moved frequently, staying mostly in boarding houses, and kept almost no property.

His first philosophical work concerned the interpretation of Descartes in his own unique geometric fashion (the *Principles of the Philosophy of René Descartes*, 1663, in Latin). It is customary to relate Spinoza to Descartes or position the two on opposing sides of a philosophical argument: Descartes the philosopher of transcendence and dualism versus Spinoza the immanent monist. But this construction can oversimplify important nuances. Descartes accepted the rule of the Church in all matters concerning value and the salvation of the soul, whereas Spinoza enlists religious terminology and passion for a new secular religion that couples reason and salvation in this world. In 1670 his *Theological-Political Treatise* was released by a fictitious publisher without the author's name. The book raises harsh questions about the way in which organized religions cultivate prejudice, irrationality, and the fear of freedom. Instead, the book offers steps to achieving enlightenment that include both practicing reason and appropriating good customs and habits that arise from tradition and institutions associated with the state.

Spinoza was eventually revealed as the author of the *Treatise*, and the "heretic Jew" became the target of extraordinary criticism from many factions. Jews, Catholics, Calvinists, and Lutherans, liberals, and Cartesians competed to condemn him the most harshly. For the rest of the seventeenth century the words *Spinozism* and *Spinozist* were used as insult and threat.

His greatest and most comprehensive work, the *Ethics,* developed over the course of his mature life as a thinker. Letters to friends in 1661 touch upon important themes from the book and mention a study group that took shape around early drafts. The ideas of the *Ethics*, however, remained hidden from mainstream society. The book famously rejects an appeal to an otherworldly reality. It denies an external creator and asserts that nature contains both the cause and explanation of itself. Such a claim could not be made public even in the moderate and liberal Dutch republic.

Deïst

Spinoza lived an ascetic life and rejected offers for financial help from his close circle of friends as well as a position of philosophy professor at the famous German university of Heidelberg. He did so to maintain his absolute freedom to think and create. He worked as a lens crafter and died at the age of forty-three—probably of a pulmonary disease. A year later his friends brought his complete writings to publication. Even though the house and place of publication remained unmentioned, the author himself received full credit.

Radical Simplicity

Many commentators mistake the secrecy associated with Spinoza's life and writings to be a feature of the texts themselves. British philosopher Stewart Hampshire holds that "Spinoza never intended to communicate his real meaning, or the more significant part of his philosophy, to his contemporaries, except a few close friends. . . . [He] believed that his contemporaries could not even try to understand his thought, because its conclusions were evidently incompatible with their deepest religious loyalties and moral prejudices. Being fully understood would cause a horrible scandal and it would destroy all tranquility in his life. In fact, he could not afford to be understood."[2]

It is indeed one of the most common claims in the literature on Spinoza. The notion that Spinoza did not want to be understood reinforces the difficulty many readers experience in accessing his writing. Spinoza is indeed difficult, but not because his writing is. His philosophy is uncompromising—it begins with a few claims we might intuitively accept and leads to positions many of us find jarring. The problem is that the transition from the one to the other follows like a logical, geometric proof. Whereas Spinoza does not shy away from the results of his strict reasoning, most readers feel that the results might be too far-fetched and feel inclined to domesticate the text by reinterpretation.

This chapter assumes a different Spinoza—a straightforward thinker who speaks freely and directly and whom we should take at face value. With this reading we can follow Spinoza in a way that challenges our own metaphysical baggage. Are we willing to accept his radical emphasis on the concreteness of life without any limits or promises of another world? If so, are we willing to accept his denial of human freedom, as it is customarily conceived? And will we follow Spinoza's logic to the point of integrating ourselves in a community of others, animate and inanimate, renouncing our individuality and our privileged position?

The first part of the *Ethics*, "On God," begins with a set of propositions:

> D3: By substance I understand what is in itself and is conceived through itself.
> D4: By attribute I understand what the intellect perceives of a substance, as constituting its essence.
> D6: By God I understand a being absolutely infinite, that is, a substance consisting of an infinity of attributes, of which each one expresses an eternal and infinite essence.

While these ideas would have been intuitively acceptable to a seventeenth-century philosopher, to us such talk of God as one substance with infinite attributes can seem a bit alienating. But the core notion is familiar: Spinoza argues for the complete identification of God and nature. "That eternal and infinite being we call God or Nature, acts from the same necessity from which he exists," he writes (IV, preface). This famous sentence—omitted from the first Dutch translation—presents the radical but intuitive premise from the outset. The single substance that exists in infinite ways—God or nature—is the totality of things in this world.

This set of definitions states the obvious: everything is everything, and there is nothing apart from it. Everything must be conceived through itself (I, D3). We can only know the whole (substance) through our limited perception (attributes) (I, D4). The totality represents "God," "Nature," or the infinite, and we—as finite beings—are modes of this infinite, all-inclusive eternal (I, D6).

The consequences of this set of assertions are surprising. Spinoza's basic intuition in the first part of the *Ethics* asserts that God cannot be separated from what is. God does not create the world but is identical to it in its totality and infinity. This view threatens organized religion, because many perceive it to downgrade God to the level of the material world. Seen a different way, Spinoza's claim is merely an elevation of nature. Both descriptions, however, are lacking since they employ a value hierarchy Spinoza rejects. The identification of God and nature creates a new concept of God and a new concept of nature on an equal, united foundation.

According to Spinoza, there is only one substance that can be approached in infinite many ways. Of these we humans know only two—extension and thought. We perceive physical entities that extend in space and we approach the world intellectually as a set of ideas or meanings. Spinoza does not stop to elaborate on our finite limitation, and there is no way of measuring what we cannot know. But humility must accompany our attempts to know the world. There is an internal, immanent limit to human knowledge, not because there is a transcendent world beyond the one we inhabit, but because this one is infinite.

Spinoza's monism lays out what philosopher Gilles Deleuze calls "a common plane of immanence on which all bodies, all minds, and all individuals, are situated."[3] All that there is, in its totality, is a continuous weave of interconnectedness. This can either sound mystical or simply self-evident: everything is everything and there is nothing else. It can also explain some of the more stupefying statements in the first part of the *Ethics* concerning the necessity of this world. In Spinoza's twenty-ninth proposition he tells us, "In nature there is nothing contingent, but all things have been determined from the necessity of the divine nature to exist and produce an effect in a certain way" (I, P29). And, as if to infuriate us even more, Spinoza continues, "Things could have been produced by God in no other way, and in no other order than they have been produced" (I, P33). On the one hand, it seems absurd that Spinoza would deny God the freedom to create the world differently. But this becomes clear if we remember that God is the totality of things. God does not play dice, as Einstein would say later.[4] This is so because God is actualized in this world by the totality of all things. He (or she or it: Spinoza repeatedly ridicules the personification of God as a kind of superhuman being) does not maintain an identity outside of this world, a platform from which to will it differently. In that respect God too is bound by the necessity of this world.

God as a willing, active agent is dropped from Spinoza's explanation: nature has no external purposes, and there are no fixed values beyond the totality of this world. But Spinoza's claim is even stronger. It affirms our existence here in the happening world and emphatically asserts, "By reality and perfection I understand the same thing" (II, D6). What exists is perfect. This does not mean that we must accept everything as it is, but that we need to view things as they are without the veil of myth, external purposes, or prejudice. The world as it is includes no judgment and no essential "good" or "evil." It is simply what it is—though viewing it as such is no simple feat. Since there is no external perspective and no "outside world" to compare this one with, we can logically conclude that it lacks nothing. It is perfect.

The Blushing Face of God

Apart from the rejection of the duality of creator and created, Spinoza rejects another famous duality—that of the mind and the body. The separation of these two is a fundamental tenet of the Judeo-Christian conception of humanity and remains strong even today, if under secular guise. According to Spinoza, mind, spirit, or soul (I use these indiscriminately to encompass a wide range of associations) is nature's self-expression. In other words, it is one of the forms of "God" or "Nature."

This notion resembles naturalism, but naturalism typically involves a further conclusion: that all the mental, spiritual, moral, or religious phenomena can be reduced to material processes. Spinoza does not share this reductive view. For him, the mental and the physical are two aspects of one and the same substance.

Humans can understand only two attributes of the world as we encounter it—extension and thought—which are parallel and equal expressions. Neither is higher and neither reduces to the other. Descartes thought the two are distinct things—a thinking thing and an extended thing—and this conclusion led to many problems. If they are distinct, how do they relate? How does a thought influence the body, and how does the body trigger thought? Where exactly is the seat of the "soul" or of "consciousness," and can the body know? These are just a few variants on the mind-body problem that haunt the dualist account like ghosts in the machine.

In the second part of the *Ethics*, "On the Nature and Origin of the Mind," Spinoza offers an alternative view that addresses some of the shortcomings of mind-body dualism. It too is jarringly simple: mentality and materiality (or thought and extension) function like adjectives in a sentence. They clarify aspects of the subject, but they need not overlap, intrude on, or originate from each other. "The order and connection of ideas is the same as the order and connection of things," Spinoza writes (II, P7). This proposition can be misleading since it prompts many readers to look for systematic relations between the two orders. But this misconception only proves the strength of the dualist mindset. We can follow Spinoza's terminology, but not the insight behind it. Perhaps thought and extension function like adjectives, but then we want to know how the two relate. This classic dualistic problem is misplaced. There is no gap between thoughts and things that must be closed by inventing some systematic relation. The two are expressions of the same. Spinoza explains this proposition by reminding us: "the thinking substance and the extended substance are one and the same substance, which is now comprehended under this attribute, now under that" (II, P7, S).

The monist must face some trouble as well. If there is only one substance, which we apprehend under two attributes, what is the status of particular things? How can we make sense of the fact that the world as we know it is made of separate and distinct objects? And how do those things—sand on the beach, flowers, you, me—relate to one another? Spinoza's answer is that they are the "modes" of the one substance. They are properties or qualities that substance can gain or lose without any substantial change. Modes are different from attributes because modes represent nonsubstantial configurations of nature. The scientific laws of nature are infinite modes (explaining the relations between material objects), and individuals are finite modes. Finite things do not exist necessarily—in other words, existence is not an essential part of their essence. Instead, finite things are modes of God or nature and represent part of the continuum of all substances that express God and nature. But it is important to remember that God or nature do not exist apart from these expressions. There is no hierarchy and no depth in Spinoza's system. Finite things are as important as God, since God exists in and through them.

What are we then? We are a blush on the face of God. As he argues, "the human mind is part of the infinite intellect of God" (II, P11, C). We are made of the one eternal substance—mind and matter—that is part of the whole; therefore, we help comprise the whole. How can we understand that? A blush is a mode. For a face to have a blush means that it acquires a particular tint. These are not two things: the face and the blush, standing in a certain relation; rather, we have a single thing, a face, and it is blushing.

Happiness Now

This conclusion offers us a glimpse of Spinoza's ethical doctrine as it comes to affirm and celebrates life in this world. After all, the book is not a metaphysical treatise, and reading it as such makes it unduly dull and difficult. Instead, the *Ethics* is a guide to leading a fulfilled and happy life. And, indeed, in concluding the book's second section, Spinoza describes four beneficial results of his philosophy:

1. It grants "complete tranquility of mind" since we come to understand "that we share in the divine nature."

According to Spinoza, the more we recognize this continuity and communal perspective, the more we extend onto the world, the more we achieve happiness, freedom, and blessedness.

2. "It teaches us what attitude we should adopt regarding fortune." Recognition of the larger continuity of the world helps make individual fortunes or misfortunes less significant.

3. It "assists in our social relations." It teaches us to be content with ourselves and frees us from harboring grudges, envy, or bitterness when we compare our fate to that of another.

4. Finally, it leads to a political commonwealth in that it at once maintains order and protects freedom.

Clearly, Spinoza wants to affect the reader, and part of his message involves spurring individual and social change. This change is not abstract or moral—it does not establish objective good and evil against a set of universal rules. Instead, it is ethical—that is, it offers a framework for the classical idea of "the good life" or happiness. The message includes several simple assertions. First, we are not separable from our relations with others and with the world. Second, there is no soul that hovers besides life or a transcendent, score-keeping God. (Likewise, neither rewards nor punishments await us in another world.) Third, the value of our actions lies in the doing itself, since life as whole has no purpose outside of itself. Finally, following this ethical route leads not only to individual happiness and peace of mind but also to a better community of individuals.

It is important to note that Spinoza does not reject a personal or subjective point of view. He only recommends learning to see things differently—*sub specie aeternitatis*—as part of a continuum or "under a certain form of eternity" (II, P44, C 2). Eternal for Spinoza is not the religious notion of the everlasting. Rather, the eternal is achieved when we move away from linear temporality, which is based on our subjective experiences and is marked by our beginning and ending. In Spinoza, eternity represents a wholesome and organic sense of transformation and perfection that affects the totality of things all at once. This state enables us to look at things beyond our subjective perspectives and experience ourselves as part of a much greater composition. My life and death mean something different for my parents, my children, the city in which I live, or from the point of view of nature as a whole. Spinoza's *Ethics* helps us move between these different levels so that we can settle within a position that sustains our happiness—not rejecting our individual being but not being locked in it.

Spinoza's monism denies the opposition between a sense of "me" and "not-me" as well as the opposition between this opposition and the assertion of a distinct individuality. It is like being immersed in a game, knowing oneself as a player but losing oneself in the totality of its dynamic relations. At those moments, which are experienced as instances rather than as stretches of progressive time, we participate in the harmony of existence. On this level of perfection our actions can be described as both necessary and free, and we experience ourselves equally as distinct and as part of a larger community. The immanent monism of the *Ethics* is about achieving this state of mind-body attunement, which includes the self and the infinity of this world. It is here that we can hear the ethical resonances of Spinoza's absolute affirmation of this world in its perfection: "By reality and perfection I understand the same thing."

The rest of the *Ethics* will tackle the difficulties that stand in the way of integrating ourselves into this larger composition. And there are many. We are educated and trained to think about ourselves as unique, separate entities, competing with others. A form of heightened individualism has taken hold, at least in Western cultures, and intensified since the time of Spinoza. It might be that recent developments—discoveries made in neurobiology or the experience of social networks—allow us to return today and realize the relevance of Spinoza to our everyday experience of living. But our cultural history, our language, as well as our economic, political, moral, and legal systems still insist on separating us from each other. This complex of forces helps explain why the *Ethics* sounds alternatively so intuitive and so alien.

Picturing the Geometric Soul

In all, Spinoza proves himself to be an acute and sensitive observer of the richness of human psychology. We can follow his formulations in their minute details or we can try to extrapolate in broad strokes, in the way that stepping back from a painting allows greater clarity in understanding the whole. The geometric design serves this purpose. It conveys graphically the idea of an ordered totality that can be accessed almost at any given moment and produce the same results. The *Ethics* thus develops to an unprecedented level the potential of a book to become an object of a meditative gaze. In this way it can be compared to a painting or a face. We have to take in the expression, character, or worldview as a whole before we observe them analytically or progressively. The geometric design, therefore, serves to integrate the individual within a whole, and it elicits the set of relations from which individual details emerge. The *Ethics* shows rather than tells the reader its one most important insight—the interweaving of all particulars into one scheme.

The great Dutch painters who were working alongside Spinoza contributed to the same great revelation. Their new realistic style of painting embodied spiritual meaning in everyday scenes that spoke directly and immediately to nonexperts. Vermeer's portraits showed the beauty of solitary housemaids, pouring milk, peering through a window, or staring straight ahead. And Rembrandt, living across the street from Spinoza, transplanted classic religious scenes onto the streets of Amsterdam. Dutch paintings from these years celebrate life in its concreteness. The textures of the garments, the shapes of the objects, and the light coming through an open window are bursting with life. These masterworks, like the *Ethics*, provide a vision of the eternal in the everyday.

The geometric method seemed adequate so long as we were considering God or the mind in a more or less abstract manner. But now that we have reached the level of human psychology, the text requires a more personal perspective. After all, the emotions are nothing if they are not "felt" somehow from within, and Spinoza's *Ethics* requires this force in order to motivate a change toward the picture of happiness it paints.

The text will therefore maintain its geometric view while relaxing the attempt to provide proofs for emotions: "Therefore, I shall treat the nature and powers of the affects, and the power of the mind over them, by the same method by which, in the preceding parts, I treated God and the mind, and I shall consider human actions and appetites just as if it were a question of lines, planes, and bodies" (III, preface).

The form of the exposition follows the function. The essential element in reaching a state of calm happiness is ascending to a position from which our emotional states are seen as lines, planes, and bodies and are experienced as an overall connected system of relations. We need to be able to take them in as a whole: not only this fear or that anger but rather what brought about this fear, what emotions and actions followed, and to whom these reactions are related. This form of explanation is not only linear or progressive but also backward, sideways, and in motion, since actions shape the position from which the past and the future are interpreted. For Spinoza, appreciating this connectivity means becoming active with respect to one's emotions, and "becoming active" means understanding the causes and the properties of our psychophysical states. In today's psychological jargon, we might say that Spinoza calls on us to own how we feel, and that means not to be carried under the sway of our immediate passions but to understand and so transform them.

For Spinoza, individual freedom is not an unexplained action without precedents or causes. Rather, freedom means the ability to act in accordance with one's situation. Freedom is not the opposite of necessity but the opposite of compulsion. It is a form of liberation—where an individual feels at one with the world, without expectation, judgment, fear, or hope.

A central feature in Spinoza's program is the replacement of the idea of a free, desiring subject with a more relational and biological form of striving, which he terms *conatus*. In the most general sense, *conatus*—or striving—is the very force of life that sustains and defines us: "Each thing, as far as it can by its own power, strives to persevere in its being" (III, P6). From the moment that a thing exists, it strives to persevere by maintaining or affirming its existence. Perseverance is more than survival, of course; survival is a necessary condition. Spinoza is realistic in asserting that whatever exists strives to exist and increase its power of existence. Taken by itself, this proposition can be misleading since it begins with "each thing" and then endows the thing with a mysterious power of striving, as if living is an extra force added to the material world. The next proposition balances this impression: "The striving by which each thing strives to persevere in its being is nothing but the actual essence of the thing" (III, P7). The form of striving that we take is who we are in essence. Here we begin correctly, with life, and it is life that takes different shapes of striving. Life individuates itself into different individuals who then express and experience themselves as different forms of striving. The form of striving is "nothing but the actual essence of the thing."

We can compare Spinoza's conatus with Freud's notion of libido, which serves to describe a similar undefined energy of life. For both thinkers (and therapists, in their different ways) we become free only when we understand and embrace this life force that shapes us. By taking responsibility for it, we make it our own. Both the therapeutic and philosophical approaches are morally neutral; their struggle is against forms of repression that restrict our libido or conatus by appealing to external or abstract set of considerations. The "good" is explained as an affirmation of existence and is expressed as an increase in activity and freedom. The more we take responsibility for our nature, the more active, free, and happy we become.

Now, as individuals, we know our form of striving only partially. But when the striving becomes self-conscious, not only of its objects but of its particular form as one form of life, it affirms its own existence. This is Spinoza's famous "intellectual love"—this desiring desire, this affirmation of affirmation, this passion that knows itself as both knowledge and love. Spinoza calls this state of happiness, perhaps ironically, after his own first name, *Benedictos* in Latin, *Baruch* in Hebrew: "the blessed one."

The Highest Desire

Self-conscious striving—the striving that strives to know itself—is Spinoza's definition of philosophy. It is the love of knowledge.

The last section of the *Ethics* returns us to the original intent of the book—to serve as a modern guide to the perplexed who want to find meaning and happiness in *this* life, rather than appeal to external causes or purposes. The book is a spiritual exercise, not a metaphysical theory: "And he who will observe these rules carefully—for they are not difficult—and practice them, will soon be able to direct most of his actions according to the command of reason" (V, P10, S).

The rules are not difficult. They consist mostly in expanding the region of knowledge and allowing us to know ourselves as one integrated mind-body, within an ever-growing environment of life. Because the knower and the known are one and the same, at the highest point our desire to know turns into love, and the love is nothing but the desire to know. To love life fully is to want to know it fully—this is our ultimate end, our highest desire: "So the ultimate end of the man who is led by reason, that is, his highest desire, by which he strives to moderate all others, is that by which he is led to conceive adequately both himself and all things which can fall under his understanding" (IV, appendix, 4).

The lover of wisdom is a lover of this world, and truly knowing oneself means experiencing oneself as interwoven into the fabric of this world. The odd couple, love and knowledge—just like the creator and the created, mind and body, or necessity and freedom— are integrated within the movement of life that the *Ethics* charts. This is why Spinoza can argue that "a free man thinks of nothing less than of death, and his wisdom is a meditation on life, not on death" (V, P67). "Meditation on life" feeds our intellectual curiosity and enriches our practical and emotional embodiment in it. It is a manifestation of what Spinoza poetically terms *intellectual love,* that is, the infinite passion to know that binds everything together.

The *Ethics* is an enveloping text. By the time we finish it, we realize that we had the vision in place long ago and that the reasoning returned, each time with a different perspective, to the same field of existence. The reading takes us progressively from one argument to the next amid the whole, which exists simultaneously like a geometric proof. With Spinoza we reach the eternal in and through time, though time itself changes with this experience. Likewise, we achieve perfection by meditating life in its concreteness and the life we encounter changes in this very process.

4

COMMUNICATING SOLITUDE

Rousseau's *Reveries of the Solitary Walker*

If the life and death of Socrates give us a portrait of what it means
to be an individual, and Spinoza adds the world in which we live
and act, then Rousseau combines the two to provide a portrait of
the individual in modern times. Rousseau confronts one of the
most contemporary of all our problems: the struggle to remain an
individual in an increasingly homogenized world and to express
oneself when all the outlets for doing so have become trite and triv-
ial. Though he was perhaps the first literary celebrity, his life was
plagued by loneliness. Already during his times, his biography and
provocative ideas were widely known. But as much as everyone
knew him, or knew about him, he remained elusive. In Rousseau
we find the seeds of a modern divide between one's inner experiences and one's public image. Rousseau struggled to bridge this
divide by writing three autobiographies. The first two—*The Con-
fessions of Jean-Jacques Rousseau* and *Dialogues: Rousseau Judge*

of Jean-Jacques—shocked the authorities and excited a recently formed public readership. He gained fame and was one of the earliest examples of the new category of "man of letters." *Reveries of the Solitary Walker* was his last attempt to provide an account of himself—the lone writer—in a manner that was at once philosophical and fundamentally personal.

Biography

Rousseau was an obsessive memoirist: his three autobiographies amounted to an unusually large number for any era, and particularly so in his time. In eighteenth-century Calvinist Europe one had to be royalty, a bishop, or at least a noble to be worthy of a book.

Rousseau was none of that. He was born in Geneva in 1712 and ✓ educated as an orthodox Calvinist. His mother died soon after giving birth, and his father abandoned him when he was ten. He was left in the care of a Protestant minister and later served as an apprentice to a tyrannical engraver. At the age of sixteen he fled Geneva and traveled throughout Europe, picking up various occupations as he went. His great love was his older patron and mistress, Madame de Warens, twelve years his elder. They met when he was sixteen—he called her Mamma and she called him Little One. But he lived most of his life with an uneducated servant who was the mother of his five children, all of whom he gave to an orphanage.

One might consider these life details to be irrelevant to the philosopher's mind and to his ideas. But Rousseau made his own life central to his texts. After all, he explains that his philosophy is not meant for others but for himself to explain and justify his existence: "I have met many men who were more learned in their philosophizing, but their philosophy remained as it were external to them. . . . They studied human nature in order to speak knowledgeably about it, not in order to know themselves. . . . For my part, when I have set out to learn something, my aim has been to gain knowledge of myself and not to be a teacher."[1]

A few pages later, he summarizes his position by saying: "Their philosophy is meant for others; I need one for myself" (*Reveries*, 53). The concept of a "personal philosophy," which is so common for us today, arose partly from the revolution Rousseau helped instigate. Rousseau was never a philosopher in the academic sense. He followed the more ancient Socratic tradition of philosophy as a way of life and an exercise in the art of living. Like Socrates, he was a plebeian whose knowledge was based in love. But unlike Socrates, who wrote nothing, Rousseau was an obsessive recorder of his own experience. He conducted his "care of the self" in the medium of writing; therefore his dialogue becomes an internal exchange within his mind or between himself, as a lone author, and a similarly solitary reader.

Rousseau was a prolific writer: an essayist, novelist, and a musician, best known for his theory of social freedom, rights, education, and religion. He achieved fame for a prize-winning essay about what benefits the arts and sciences conferred on mankind (1750). His novel argument was that, contrary to the position of the Enlightenment, arts and sciences do not benefit mankind; rather, they create wants, and wants enslave man. These ideas were elaborated in the "Discourse on Inequality" (1754), in which he famously asserted that "man is naturally good, and only by institutions is he made bad." The idea that we are born good and are gradually corrupted is an ironic reversal of the doctrine of original sin and salvation through the Church.

In 1760 he published his novel *Julie* (*La Nouvelle Héloîs*); and in 1762, *Émile*—a treatise on education—and *The Social Contract*, which became his most important philosophical works. They achieved such enormous success that they were regarded as dangerous to the political order and to the Church. Like Socrates, Rousseau was accused of introducing a new, unorthodox religion. The accusations leveled against him by the Paris parliamentarians bear an uncanny resemblance to the accusations against Socrates, and they also reveal the general inquietude certain philosophers are able to generate. The judgment describes Rousseau as "asserting blasphemous, ungodly, and detestable principles, containing indecent material offensive to propriety and modesty, together with propositions subversive to sovereign authority, setting forth maxims of education which could only produce men devoted to skepticism and toleration, abandoned to their passions, men given over to the pleasures of the senses."[2]

To a modern audience this kind of condemnation from the ruling majority might as well be put on the back cover of the book as an endorsement. But to Rousseau this controversy did not constitute a marketing ploy. Instead, it forced him to flee Continental Europe. Eventually he ended up in England as a guest of the Scottish philosopher David Hume, where he had great social success and was granted a pension by George III. But fame, as we know from our own celebrity culture, carries a toll. Rousseau became suspicious and accused Hume of plotting against him. He fled to Paris and wrote his autobiographies before dying in extreme poverty.

From these pages Rousseau emerges as a truly unique individual: funny, outrageous, extravagant, original, exposed, and yet sensitive and susceptible to the views of others. His writings highlight the tension between the human desire to love and be loved, on the one hand, and the opposing need to maintain a sense of independence and individual autonomy. This tension appears in the *Reveries* as the conflict between solitude and society and the uncompromising self that yearns for understanding and communion. In almost all Rousseau's writings he attempts to restore a symbiotic state of natural harmony while maintaining individual freedom.

A Book for No One and Everyone

Rousseau began what was to be his last book in the autumn of 1776, when he was sixty-four years old. The last entry was written in 1778. One month later Rousseau accepted the invitation of a rich admirer and moved to his estate near Paris. He went on a morning walk but came home unexpectedly early. He died soon after, leaving the *Reveries* as his last, unfinished work.

The *Reveries* is a very peculiar work. It is genre bending, eluding the distinctions between philosophy and literature, fiction, and biography. At times it seems like the work of an aging madman suffering from persecution mania. But it is also the work of a thinker coming of age, collecting his life into a heartfelt, albeit idiosyncratic, memoir. The literary nature of the work is inseparable from its intimacy, expressiveness, and ability to achieve clarity about itself. In this Rousseau offers us another example of what we call the life of philosophy.

The opening line is a perfect example of Rousseau's particular mix of personal pathos and philosophical acuity: "So now I am alone in the world" (*Reveries*, 27). It is a dramatic beginning, no doubt, and one that quickly establishes an unusual connection to the reader of this work. As readers, we are excluded from the book because the author tells us that he is alone in the world. And yet we are brought closer because, like the solitary writer, we are reading alone. We are at once too far away and too close. Is this a double voice, one that calls for our attention at the same time that it makes it impossible? Or perhaps this is the very condition of writing (and reading), which creates intimacy between utter strangers? Writing and reading, as the opening sentence makes clear, is a shared experience that is also one of isolation.

Rousseau employs his solitude as an opportunity to discover who he really is: "But I, detached as I am from them and from the whole world, what am I? This must now be the object of my inquiry" (*Reveries*, 27). We cannot avoid the feeling that these words are intended for our ears. Is he feigning solitude, or is this "detachment" sincere? How can an author write a book without at least imagining a reader? A diary writer, for example, always contemplates the idea of an outside reader, even if she never intents to publish her words. We are all familiar with this paradox: we write only for ourselves, but somehow there is someone else present, looking over our shoulder. What is this insistence of "the other" that creeps into our most intimate moments of self-reflection? Is it the power of language or the effect of writing? After all, my words are never my own—I did not invent this sentence but only appropriated it. Language is a borrowed tool, and that's partly why it's so handy.

Likewise, reading involves this double play between solitude and communication. Reading the *Reveries*, one hears one's own voice reflected back from the page—"So now I am alone in the world." This sentence starts midway, as if continuing an inner conversation that rings in my ear. The voice of the author shapes the inner voice heard by the reader. The doubling of oneself in writing and in reading represents the intimacy of solitary individuals and becomes a way of communicating solitude.

Varieties of Loneliness

It has been mentioned before that the beginning line, "So now I am alone in the world" is reminiscent of Descartes's "Ego cogito ergo sum" ("I think therefore I am").[3] The resonance comes fully in the French: Rousseau's "Me voici donc seule" picks up on Descartes's famous assertion, which translates into French as "Je pense donc je suis." The story of Descartes's realization is well known. Attempting to find an absolute certainty, he starts by methodologically doubting whatever he can. He dismisses the evidence of the senses and proceeds to more extreme, hyperbolic, skeptical arguments regarding hallucinations, madness, dreams, and a deceptive God. From the senses to mathematics, everything can be doubted, and only one thing remains. "I am, I exist, is necessarily true whenever it is put forward by me or conceived in my mind."[4] According to this reasoning, as long as I meditate, I exist, even though the essence of this existence and whatever I know about the world might be wrong. The fact of existence remains always beyond the possibility of doubt. The *Cogito*, as the argument is commonly known, is therefore the bedrock of certainty on which the edifice of knowledge can be erected.

Rousseau is not interested in objective certainty but in knowing how he is detached from everyone else. His method is not doubt but existential isolation—a mental exercise that makes others disappear: "For now they are strangers and foreigners to me; they no longer exist for me, since this is their will." And the crucial question then arises, which is worth repeating here again: "But I, detached as I am from them and from the whole world, what am I?" (*Reveries*, 27).

Descartes proceeds in similar fashion but arrives at a different result. To the question "What am I?" he undoubtedly responds, I am "a thing that thinks. What is that? A thing that doubts, understands, affirms, denies, is willing, is unwilling, and also imagines and has sensory perceptions" (Second Meditation, 28). That is not Rousseau's answer. Thinking about thinking is not his way of achieving certainty. In fact, it causes a greater confusion: "the more I think about my present situation, the less I can understand what has become of me" (*Reveries*, 27). The *Reveries*, as the term indicates, is not a conscious attempt to achieve the clarity of thinking. Rather, it is a way of releasing one's thinking, drawing on the imagination, and investigating oneself as an experiencing subject, outside the influence of others and, as much as possible, prior to language.

"These pages," he tells either himself or his presumed reader, "will be no more than a formless record of my reveries. . . . I shall say what I have thought just as it comes to me, with little connection as the thoughts of this morning have with those of last night" (*Reveries*, 32). By pledging not to censor himself, Rousseau offers the record of his sincere self-examination. Rousseau goes as far as comparing it to a "barometer reading of my soul" (*Reveries*, 33). Since we cannot be present as readers, this record can only serve the author himself, a way of commemorating his existence and making friends with himself: "in writing them . . . I shall as it were double the space of my existence, and in my decrepitude I shall live with my earlier self as I might with a younger friend" (*Reveries*, 34).

Rousseau's solitary *Cogito* can also be compared to a more removed assertion—Abraham's response "Here I am" [הנני] to God's call to sacrifice Isaac. Abraham's response expresses the existential solitude of man facing the invisible demand of God. His "Here I am" is traditionally interpreted as the representation of absolute submission or faith. God calls on him to perform the impossible—to sacrifice his son—and he asks no questions and expresses no doubt. It is the polar opposite of Descartes's "I think therefore I am." The *Cogito* is absolute trust in one's own independent thinking, and the Abrahamic "Here I am" is absolute trust in a power beyond oneself.

Rousseau holds the paradoxical middle between these two extremes. His opening line is both an attempt to rely solely on himself and a realization of the absolute dependence of the self on others. Like Descartes, Rousseau searches for his true self—his existence as an individual human being. His experience of loneliness takes the shape of contemplative solitude and finds its voice in writing. Following Abraham, Rousseau's cry is tormented and conflicted: it renounces external knowledge and affirms faith. "So I am alone" is a moment of clarity and of obscurity. It brings the self back to itself, to the certainty of one's experience, as well as fracturing it such that one's self is infused with otherness.

Friendship

Devoid of all companionship, Rousseau transforms the classic demand to "examine oneself" into a more modern project of becoming friends with oneself: "I shall take the barometer readings of my soul. . . . When the time for my departure draws near, I shall recall in reading them the pleasure I have in writing them and by thus reviving times past I shall as it were double the space of my existence . . . I shall live with my earlier self as I might with a young friend" (*Reveries*, 33–34).

By writing himself, he is able to double "the space of my existence" as if the record left in writing will allow the older Rousseau to enjoy his younger self. The interesting fact is that the very act of recording the experience already anticipates the future reading, and so the doubling of existence is achieved in the present. As we mentioned, the act of writing here and now anticipates a reading in some other time and place. Therefore, the relationship between the biographical "I" in the text and the author who creates that text is never easy or harmonious. The two are not identical. And the *Reveries* is outstanding not because of this inherent difference, which is true for all biographies, but because it lets us see the difference. The thoughts and events Rousseau narrates show more of the person than what the author intends. For instance, while the author asserts his renunciation of the human race, we can sense his yearning for social connection, growing paranoia, and desire to control and shape his public image. At times we wish to protect Rousseau, the person, from the text Rousseau the author lays. We see him cause harm to himself, and we wish to correct him for his own benefit. At times this peculiar text puts us in the odd position of knowing more or better than the author about himself.

In *The Social Contract* Rousseau distinguishes between two kinds of relations one can have toward oneself: a beneficial one, arising from the state of nature, and a restrictive one, resulting from the corruption of society. The first, *amour de soi meme*, is necessary for personal happiness and enhances one's well-being among others. The second, *amour propre*, arises from comparing oneself with others and imposing standards of excellence that are alien to one's own nature. Friendship with oneself is a way of returning to natural self-love and rejecting the conditions of social alienation. The condition of solitude allows Rousseau to reflect on himself without comparisons or judgment, and this reflection resembles a mature form of *amour de soi meme*. For Rousseau, the consequences are not only personal happiness but also harmony with others. This could be Rousseau's ethical imperative—write yourself such that you would be the person you would enjoy meeting again in your older years.

Achieving this imperative is no small task, and it could come at the expense of friendships with others. Rousseau is not unaware of this risk. Like Socrates, Rousseau positions himself as living outside the norms of his society, and outside his times—but also as representing the most basic human tendencies. His condition of being utterly alone is one that all of us share, particularly when reading or writing. His claim to be completely unique is, ironically, what each of us feels. Our inability to communicate our inner self and our craving for such communicability is captured, most precisely, by this "most peculiar human being that has ever lived." With Rousseau individual intimacy is not separated from universal communicability because we are all intimate and inaccessible in the same way.

Both Socrates and Rousseau are outstanding human beings because they are just that and nothing more—human beings. After all, the hardest thing is to just be what one is. They are not divine or mystical and they do not posses any special wisdom. This is what distinguishes the practice of philosophy from other religious, poetic, or doctrinal practices. Its role models are not saints, geniuses, or enlightened individuals but very earthy ones. They wear their faults—Socrates' vanity, Rousseau's excessive self-pity and self-love—plainly on their sleeves. We care about these individuals. We can be their friends because they are individuals and we are placed in a position to continue their project of the "care of the self" not because they completed it to perfection but because they did not.

Rousseau's Method of Self-Examination: The Reveries

Rousseau's self-examination is not intended to yield an abstract theory but a new relationship with himself that extends his existence and establishes a friendship within it. Achieving this goal requires a unique form of experiencing and an original form of writing that corresponds with experience. Rousseau calls both by the same name, *reveries,* because they are two dimensions of the same process.

The walks, which are more like strolls than goal-oriented exercises, create an opportunity for a *wandering of the soul*. They bring about a state of freedom in which thoughts move freely without the requirement of reaching a certain objective. More than daydreaming or hallucinating, a reverie is the process of thinking profoundly (*penser profondement*), such that a thought sinks into itself and discovers its different voices and forms. Thinking becomes much richer when we stop using it as a tool for practical gains. Reveries, therefore, are a way of embodying thinking fully and appreciating its imaginative and emotional dimensions. A reverie, in Rousseau's conception, is a certain way of thinking that refuses to give up the richness of meaning for the sake of order and systematization. Inherently a solitary endeavor, it's a way of noting the movement of experience, the thoughts and sensations that go by while drifting with the flow of life. This may sound similar to some schools of Eastern meditation, and, indeed, Rousseau's reveries at times suggest the calmness and peace of mind of meditational practices. But it is dissimilar in the sense that reveries serve a particular philosophical purpose—a way of achieving happiness and calmness not just here and now for the solitary self but communicating this state and sharing it with others.

Reveries imply communication, even if their communication is first an inner dialogue within oneself. Rousseau wishes to keep a "faithful record" without restricting his wandering thoughts. But here he encounters an obstacle: how can he document his thoughts without thereby transforming them or restricting their freedom? "Surrounded by such riches, how was I to keep a faithful record of them all? As I tried to recall so many sweet reveries, I relived them instead of describing them. The memory of this state is enough to bring it back to life; if we completely ceased to experience it, we should soon lose all knowledge of it" (*Reveries*, 36). The problem is simple enough: if you live your experiences, you cannot write them, and if you write them then you are not living in the present. It is impossible to write from inside an experience, since the writing will evidently change the experience; and it is impossible to write from outside an experience because the writer is distanced from it. Rousseau captures the fundamental tension between writing and experiencing by acknowledging that the intimacy of experience is exactly what escapes representation.

Why then try at all? Why try to put my intimacy into words? The answer here has to do with the fact that having an experience partly implies being able to share it with others. Experience itself involves a movement toward communication. We can notice this in certain extreme situations, usually when communication itself is restricted because of internal or external circumstances. Take the experience of beauty, for example. When we listen to a beautiful piece of music, we immediately want to share it, even though the very thing we want to share—the beauty of the music—is exactly what can't be explained. When I find beauty in a painting, I want to point at it and share it with others. I can talk about the colors or the shape; I can mention the history of art and the biography of the painter. But what is most special about this—beauty itself—escapes representation. In the case of beauty, the desire to share is clearly felt because it is never fully satisfied. Beauty is what we want to share and feel unable to, a fact that makes the desire to communicate all the more visceral.

The experience of art might be a special case, because it pushes communication to its limit. But communicability is a dimension of every experience. In a certain sense, experience is never absolutely solitary since it includes the drive to share it with others. Rousseau reveals the working of that impulse since in his case it persists even though there is no one else around.

Rousseau's *Reveries* are an attempt to communicate experience without reliving or killing it. It is here that *Reveries* become a literary experiment in self-expression—in the writing of the self. In his reading of the *Reveries*, philosopher Eli Friedlander claims that the book itself can be read as an allegory of writing: "in reading the *Reveries* it is easy to miss the fact that writing itself is Rousseau's foremost concern. He writes about the writing of his reveries: not the experiences or the reveries it triggers, but rather what it is to recollect them in writing." Therefore, Friedlander concludes, "writing is the fundamental activity in the *Reveries*, and all else, all the other activities Rousseau engages in, are allegories of that writing, and therefore also allegories of reading that text" (*An Afterlife of Words*, 16–7).

This emphasis on writing is crucial for understanding Rousseau's *Reveries*. Rousseau writes about the writing of experience and the difficulties of doing so. The *Reveries* serve as a bridge between experience and language, writing and life. The project here is to make experience and writing come together so that it is possible to write oneself by way of experiencing oneself or to experience oneself by way of writing. And if Rousseau is successful, then he can be assured that the writing will not alienate him from his experiences or become a lifeless transcription. In the *Reveries* experience and the writing of experience are two manifestations of the same underlying activity.

Reconstructing Experience

The continuum between writing and life is perhaps most pronounced in the Second Walk. Our hero is attacked by a Great Dane and knocked unconscious. Neither fully conscious nor unconscious, Rousseau describes his awakening from the fall:

Night was coming on. I saw the sky, some stars, and a few leaves. This first sensation was a moment of delight. I was conscious of nothing else. In this instant I was being born again, and it seemed as if all I perceived was filled with my frail existence. Entirely taken up by the present, I could remember nothing; I had no distinct notion of myself as a person, nor had I the least idea of what had just happened to me. I did not know who I was, nor where I was; I felt neither pain, fear, nor anxiety. I watched my blood flowing as I might have watched a stream, without even thinking that the blood had anything to do with me. I felt throughout my whole being such a wonderful calm, that whenever I recall this feeling I can find nothing to compare with it in all the pleasures that stir our lives.

(Reveries, 39)

As Rousseau regains his consciousness, he cannot fully distinguish between himself and the world. In this awakening he is reborn, and the world is born with him. His awareness is entirely claimed by the present, and a perfect calm dawns upon him as he watches his own blood flowing like a stream.

This awakening transports him, and the reader is transported with him through his prose. Individual objects lose their distinctness. As consciousness merges with the unconscious, the physical world unites with the body, and the reader comes into this orbit as well. But inasmuch as this is a condition of rebirth or resurrection, it is also, weirdly, an experience of utmost alienation. Rousseau describes himself as elevated and disembodied from his experiential self: "I watched my blood flowing as I might have watched a stream, without even thinking that the blood had anything to do with me" (*Reveries*, 39). The continuity between himself and the world is simultaneously the most extreme case of self-estrangement.

Even more striking, these eloquent descriptions of his accident—and the ecstasy and confusion it entailed—were constructed from secondhand reports he heard afterwards. Rousseau does not hide this fact. Instead, he acknowledges it as he describes his awakening: "I was in the arms of two or three men who told me what had happened" (*Reveries*, 38). And he does so again after detailing the incident: "So much I learned from those who had picked me up and were still holding me when I came to" (*Reveries*, 39). The elegance of his prose often hides these small caveats, and as readers we tend to fall for the "authenticity" and "originality" of his writing. However the most intimate experience of inner peace and self-contentment is not even his own; it is a fiction constructed after the event.

This rebuilding of events is not necessarily a lie. On the contrary, what Rousseau shows is that a textual recreation is inherent to experience as such. Experience is never wholly present in one moment. It is an extension of our being over time. To have an experience means being able to recollect it, and this recollection is always a reconstruction from hindsight. The dog's attack only dramatizes the fact that experience is always already mediated, and this mediation occurs through language.

The reveries, as a textual genre, bridge this duality. They involve both simple, unobstructed experiences and the marks left by those experiences upon subsequent reflection. The majority of the text focuses not on the reconstruction that is inherent to experience but on an immediate "presentness." This might seem confusing until we are reminded that this is a text and that the immediacy described is always achieved in and through mediation—such as the example of Rousseau's stay on the island of Saint-Pierre, described in the Fifth Walk:

But if there is a state where the soul can find a resting-place secure enough to establish itself and concentrate its entire being there, with no need to remember the past or reach into the future, where time is nothing to it, where the present runs on indefinitely but this duration goes unnoticed, with no sign of the passing of time, and no other feeling of deprivation or enjoyment, pleasure or pain, desire or fear than the simple feeling of existence, a feeling that fills our soul entirely, as long as this state lasts, we can call ourselves happy. . . . Such is the state which I often experienced on the Island of Saint-Pierre. In my solitary reveries, whether I lay in a boat and drifted where the water carried me, or sat by the shores of the stormy lake, or elsewhere, on the banks of a lovely river or a stream murmuring over the stones.

(Reveries, 88–89)

This description, which conjures up waves gently rocking the drifting boat, tempts us to believe that a reverie is nothing more than a state wherein the mind flows continuously with its surroundings and, in the process, achieves happiness. Time "runs on indefinitely," but even this duration "goes unnoticed." Living contently in the present is a way of achieving the eternal. As Wittgenstein writes, "eternal life belongs to the one who lives in the present."[5] By immersing ourselves in the present, we merge with the flow of existence. When we are in perfect harmony with the world, time runs without notice, effortlessly.

But this flowing rumination of the soul, which Rousseau describes, is only half the story. The other side involves the textual construction of this experience. It is hard to bring to words the wonder of our existence. But this difficulty is for the philosopher a challenge and a calling. Note that the long quote just given goes on effortlessly for thirteen lines without a period to separate the sentences. It forms a wavelike stream and rocks us in its cradle. At the end of the Fifth Walk Rousseau will admit that he might not have had this experience at all, but rather dreamed it into being and put it into words.

The Book of Life

In the Seventh Walk Rousseau reflects on how nature informs his reflections on his life. He wonders why he is so drawn to botany— "why this particular activity should attract me and what charm I can find in a fruitless study where I neither make any progress nor learn anything useful" (*Reveries*, 106). As he gradually discovers, collecting plants lays a foundation for reflection and reverie. Gathering and classifying these fragments of nature prompts him to meditate on a "natural order" and to appreciate the complex interweaving of natural beings that unites humans with the world. Ironically, he discovers this unity by employing an arbitrary system of classification that subdivides and orders species according to arcane Latin names.

Botany is, of course, another way of writing life. And the book Rousseau plans to write (about "each blade of grass," as he tells us) is the book of life. What distinguishes Rousseau's exploration of nature from that of the scientist is that he does not want to *know* nature for theoretical or practical purposes. His botanical excavations involve focusing on nature and lavishing small, caring gestures upon it through the marking of language.

Life and language come together not because they are one but because of the movement of reverie that relates them. This is not a simple fusion; the tension is palpable and the problem is always alive. But the project is nevertheless not to speak over but to give voice to what remains silent and apart. As the poet Rainer Maria Rilke writes: "I hold this to be the highest task of a bond between two people: that each should stand guard over the solitude of the other. . . . Once the realization is accepted that even between the closest human beings infinite distance continues to exist, a wonderful living side by side can grow up, if they succeed in loving the distance between them which makes it possible for each to see the other whole and against a wide sky."[6] Accepting and embracing the distance makes love and friendship possible. When I think I know you, I wrong you. When I resign myself to the impossibility of knowledge, I wrong you. But when I live this tension, making it formative of our relations, I see you "whole and against a wide sky."

This tension operates between the author and the written self and between the text and the reader. Thus a book that begins by asserting its isolation ends up *making* friends.

5

HOW WE BECOME WHAT WE ARE

Nietzsche's *Genealogy of Morals*

The *Genealogy of Morals* is a feast for a philosopher. In Nietzsche's telling, it is the philosopher who guides the production of a meaningful world. Nietzsche's view of philosophy is grander than Plato's. The latter had philosophy rule the political order, whereas according to Nietzsche philosophy shapes the material of life into a beautiful and interesting existence. Moreover, the book includes wonderfully comic insights and commentary about why the philosopher should never marry or have kids, for example, or why thinkers have a taste for desert landscapes or the reasons why San Marco's Square in Venice is the best place to do your thinking, but only before noon. Part of the point of the book is to take philosophy back from the heights of abstraction to the everyday where thinking is alive—where it smells, hurts, provokes, and gives joy.

The problem for Nietzsche is what to do with desire—specifically the watered-down desire we experience in modern times, crippled by generations of social taming and the growing belief that there is not much we can do as individuals to change our world. To a large extent our desires must be modified or denied so that we can live together in today's world. In Nietzsche's terms we learn how not to desire. But that too is a form of desire—the desire not to desire. Nietzsche fears the nihilistic attitude that spreads like a digital virus when we are left without our passions. This is the problem of our times—knowledge and love come apart to such an extent that the more we know the less we care about life. Nietzsche's question is how to renew our passionate engagement with knowing the world. *The Genealogy of Morals* reveals our agency in creating meanings and values. It tells the history of the formation of our moral concepts. By showing how they came into being, it allows for creative reevaluation.

Introduction to Nietzsche

Nietzsche remains the world's best-selling and most widely known philosopher. He was born in 1844 in a small town in the Prussian province of Saxony. His father was a Protestant pastor who died when Nietzsche was four and left Nietzsche in the care of his mother and older sister. Nietzsche trained as a classicist and a *philologist*, which means, "a lover of words," a profession that has disappeared today. His achievement and brilliance were such that he was appointed professor at the university in Basel before he even received his doctorate at the astonishingly early age of twenty-four.

Nietzsche was never attracted to grand systems of philosophy such as Aristotle's or Kant's and was more interested in issues of culture, morality, and art. His unsystematic approach is encapsulated in one of his more famous statements: "God is dead." The thought is presented in a number of books, always as a hypothesis, a thought-experiment, or an event whose meaning is metaphorical rather than literal. What Nietzsche called "the death of god" was at once a cultural event that involved the demise of the Christian-moral interpretation of life and a philosophical event, which entailed abandoning absolute truth or the absolutist foundations that had dominated Western philosophy since Plato. As a cultural event, it was a source of both excitement and concern. Nietzsche feared the "nihilistic rebound" that would arise if no "life affirming" approach could take its place. As a philosophical event, the casting away of absolutism and the emphasis on individual perspective opened the way for a radical reconsideration of human existence. After his writing shattered beliefs in fixed foundations or absolute truths, the concepts of *knowledge, value, morality,* had to be rethought. Nietzsche's method and orientation in refuting accepted "truths" opened the way to a radical new thinking that shaped the history of ideas.

Nietzsche's literary career was short but very prolific. In the twenty years of his productive life, he wrote more than twenty-two books, all of which exhibit literary flare and signs of a radically provocative mind. In 1889 he was declared insane, and he died eleven years later in 1900.

Introduction to the Book

On the Genealogy of Morals, subtitled "a polemic," is considered Nietzsche's most influential and brilliant work. It is composed of three essays, all of which deal with the origins of moral values and ideals. Nietzsche takes an unorthodox perspective in relating a history of morality with the aim of establishing the value of morality to life: "have they [value judgments] hitherto hindered or furthered human prosperity?"[1] The first essay contrasts the morality of "the slave" and that of "the master," the second essay considers "guilt" and "bad conscience," and the third addresses the ascetic ideal or the self-mastery of the self. In all three cases Nietzsche seems to take pleasure in overturning the common moral assumptions. First-time readers are usually impressed with the shocking revelation that our moral standards are borrowed from the "slaves" rather than from the heroic "masters." As descendent of the slave revolt against the masters, we value moderation and selflessness rather than the triumphant celebration of desire.

According to editor Walter Kaufmann in his introduction to Nietzsche's Genealogy, "The most common misunderstanding of the book is surely to suppose that Nietzsche considers slave morality, the bad conscience, and ascetic ideals evil; that he suggests that mankind would be better off if only these things had never appeared; and that he glorifies unconscionable brutes."[2] Such widespread misconceptions are a consequence of taking Nietzsche at face value without considering his method of philosophizing. Nietzsche describes his own method in *Ecce Homo* as "philosophizing with a hammer": he begins with a radical assault on our common belief system and proceeds by exposing the ultimate artificiality of every belief system, including his own. The first step is explicit in the book, as the story turns our moral values on their head. The second step—appreciating the artifice of the moral framework—is left to the reader. The story Nietzsche tells is not intended to be swallowed as "truth," but rather as an example that what we take to be true depends on the strength of the stories we tell. Nietzsche prompts a trajectory of thinking that allows us to recreate ourselves. So the question is not to identify the values we hold and assess them as objectively good or bad. Rather, the question is why are we holding these values. How do we use them? And are they good or bad with respect to our lives as a whole?

The Impossibility of Self-Knowledge

The problem of self-knowledge appears at the very beginning of the *Genealogy:* "We are unknown to ourselves, we men of knowledge—and with good reason. We have never sought ourselves—how could it happen that we should ever *find* ourselves?" (preface, 1) Nietzsche does not mean that "we are unknown to ourselves" because we were not searching in the right place or in the right way; his argument is rather that there is an inherent impossibility in the notion of self-knowledge. "So we are *necessarily* strangers to ourselves, we do not comprehend ourselves, for us the law 'Each is further from himself' applies to all eternity—we are not 'men of knowledge' with respect to ourselves," he goes on to argue. This point is both an existential problem—that we can never know ourselves—and a way out of an existential conundrum. The failure of self-knowledge is inherent in our existence, and we are those creatures who are, for "all eternity," unknown to ourselves.

Why can't we come to know ourselves? And, if indeed that is the case, then how do we answer the Delphic call to "know thyself?" A clue is already embedded in the opening paragraph. According to Nietzsche, we are always so immersed in ourselves that we repeatedly fail to take hold of ourselves; we wake up, as it were, a split second too late:

Present experience has, I am afraid, always found us "absent minded": we cannot give our heart to it—not even our ears! Rather, as one divinely preoccupied and immersed in himself into whose ear the bell has just boomed with all its strength the twelve beats of noon suddenly starts up and asks himself: "what really was that which just struck?" so we sometimes rub our ears *afterward* and ask, utterly surprised and disconcerted, "what really was that which we have just experienced?" and moreover: "who *are* we really?" and, afterward as aforesaid, count the twelve trembling bell-stroke of our experience, our life, our *being*—and alas! miscount them.

(Preface, 1)

There is an inherent *belatedness* in our relations to ourselves. We always come to know ourselves as something already past and we cannot catch glimpse of ourselves in the present. Whatever we know of ourselves is already a shadow, a memory, or a reflection. We appear as ghosts, always vanishing or disappearing.

Nietzsche's own style mimics the very absentmindedness he speaks about. His rhetoric has a certain melody to it: it's hard to stop reading even when the exact meaning is not entirely digestible on first review. There is a force that moves inside the text, a bit like conceptual rhyming. It promises that the meaning will come into relief only later. Like a piece of music, the book's opening carries us forward, and only afterward will we discover what it was that in fact played in our ears. In reading Nietzsche we cannot stop and parse every sentence for literal meaning in the same way that we cannot stop a musical performance to probe its elements. The whole makes its sense as a form of weaving, continuously in time, and not through a systematic construction of elements.

As the opening paragraph argues, our relations to ourselves are not only that of knowledge; there are aspects and dimensions of ourselves that are hidden in darkness, not because they comprise our mystical core but because they are in constant flux. They are part of the process of making meaning rather than the produce made. The beginning attunes us to listen to the working in the work. We must have ears for Nietzsche as well as a nose.

Perspectivism

Our knowledge of ourselves is always partial because we *are* ourselves, and we cannot see around ourselves. For this reason the desire to know is particularly troubling when it focuses on the self. After all, we are closest to ourselves, which makes self-knowledge both a constant temptation and a threat.

The process of saying "I" already positions me as something other than myself. But what I want to understand is not myself as a distant object, but myself as an agent of knowledge. If I were to write a book about myself, I could try to make it comprehensive by including a full description of my body, a complete account of my mental states, and minute detail about every life experience, but the "I" who writes this book will curiously be absent. Knowledge has both an active and a passive side. The written self is like a marionette operated by forces outside the stage. Nietzsche takes a somewhat extreme position on this when he flatly denies the existence of anything but active knowledge—that the version of the self recorded in text is nothing but a fiction, created by the writer who remains in the dark. "There is no 'being' behind doing, effecting, becoming; 'the doer' is merely a fiction added to the deed—the deed is everything" (I, 13).

We should be careful to note that a "fiction" in Nietzsche's sense is not simply a falsehood. Fictions are effective in triggering experience, and they can elicit a reality that later renders them true. Declarations or promises work in this way. When I promise that "I will be different," I am committing myself to a future state and enacting a transformation in the present. Nietzsche's model for knowledge is in many ways the same. We create meanings and values by declarative statements that are verified by other declarative statements made from other points of view. For Nietzsche, the more we say "this is so," the more it actually becomes what we say. We tend to reproduce the same stories, which give the fiction a sense of objectivity because it becomes constant through repetition. Our predominant interpretations take the shape of reality because we forget the magical act of creation, and this oversight causes the final product to seem like fact.

Nietzsche refers to this view that reality consists only of interpretations as "perspectivism." According to perspectivism, there are no fixed objects, no absolute facts, no world "as it is in itself," but only viewpoints. Nietzsche did not clarify whether he embraced the full scope of this claim or whether he intended it on a conceptual level. In other words, is objective reality irrelevant, or are the meanings we ascribe to it always open to revision? And perhaps the claim is not meant to be either true or false. Perhaps it is an ethical-artistic provocation that challenges us not to accept the world as it is, but to operate in it as if the material world needed to be shaped according to our desires and projects.

Regardless of the author's intention, we must concentrate on the force and relevance of the claim today. Perspectivism has become so ingrained in contemporary mindsets that its logic seems almost mundane and the text nearly juvenile, with intellectual-sounding aphorisms such as "there is no 'being' behind doing"—a wordier variant of the commonplace "it's all relative." The view that everything is an interpretation has become our new dogma—itself a kind of truth that stands beyond interpretation. It follows from the fall of the belief in absolute truth but, ironically, it preserves the very structure of this belief in an opposite valence. When asserted as truth, perspectivism ends in self-contradiction. The paradox is, of course, that perspectivism itself must be an interpretation that lacks the power to trump other belief systems. So how is it better than any other dogma of the past?

As the contemporary American philosopher Alexander Nehamas explains, perspectivism presents a problem for the reader of Nietzsche. Though Nietzsche discusses it in his work, he seems to hold it as if his belief in it is immune from the very perspectivism it preaches.[3] All the philosophers discussed so far have raised paradoxes: Socrates focused on the knowledge that knows its lack, Spinoza coupled freedom and necessity in the form of intellectual love, and Rousseau addressed the communication of solitary experience. In the case of Nietzsche, the paradox is how to establish the validity of perspectivism as a claim. Can one believe that it is all open to interpretation without contradicting oneself or becoming dogmatic? This is not just a philosophical problem regarding the truth of a certain position. It is also a question of how we live our lives. How do we proceed today, after the death of God, without absolute foundations, and with the knowledge that meanings are ours to make? How can we believe in the validity of what we know to be our own creation? Where is the balance that gives us freedom to create meaning without falling into a void of "it's all just interpretations?" Is there a way of avoiding dogmatism, on the one hand, and nihilism on the other?

This problem is even more pronounced today, as two dogmas dominate: one religious and the other liberal-relative. For the most part, the liberal West subscribes to the belief of "live and let live" and thinks of itself as openminded and tolerant. But the one thing that liberalism tends to exclude is tolerance for those who reject pluralism. Living in a pluralistic society, we tend to think that we can accept every faith, as long as each faith respects its alternatives. But liberalism excludes those belief systems that cannot accept this requirement. In so doing, it forgets that it too is motivated by a certain belief—the belief in the value of pluralism. But that is exactly what the nonliberal world does not wish to accept. Pluralism is a practice and a choice that most of us think is preferable. But it is a choice that excludes the dominance of tradition, family, or the search for a meaning that requires unity rather than individualism. The problem of liberalism follows from a perspectival mindset that makes itself immune to a perspectivist evaluation. On the other hand, true open-mindedness must begin by recognizing our own belief system, the lifestyle it elevates, and the ones that it excludes. Recognizing our belief system does not necessarily involve changing it. On the contrary, it is only then that we can, for the first time, chose it for ourselves.

Master and Slave

In section 3 of the introduction, Nietzsche explains how he came to investigate the field of morality. It was his sense of suspicion and disbelief that led him to question "all that has hitherto been celebrated on earth as morality" (preface, §3). Truths that proclaim themselves beyond evaluation or interpretation are the most potent seductions because, at the outset, they defy critical examination. As he explains in the *Will to Power*: "The view that *truth is found* and that ignorance and error are at an end is one of the most potent seductions there is. Supposing it is believed, then the will to examination, investigation, caution, experimentation is paralyzed: it can even count as criminal, namely as *doubt* concerning truth—'Truth' is therefore more fateful than error and ignorance, because it cuts off forces that work toward enlightenment and knowledge."[4] The purpose of *The Genealogy of Morals*, as Nietzsche tells us, is to uncover "under what conditions did man devise these value judgments, good and evil? *and what value do they themselves possess?*" (preface, §3). The essence of value judgments can be revealed by understanding "the conditions and circumstances in which they grew, under which they evolved and changed" (preface, §6). If examined in its historical context, morality itself will no longer appear as an objective truth, but rather as a result or a response to situation-based forces— "morality as consequence, as symptom, as mask, as tartufferie, as illness, as misunderstanding" (preface, §6). Morality is a fiction we come to accept as truth. It therefore shapes our perspective, molds our views, and situates us as individuals in the world. The genealogical wheel turns again, making morality not only an effect of forces but also a force in itself that shapes further development: "morality as cause, as remedy, as stimulant, as restraint, as poison" (preface, §6).

Nietzsche is a master in ringing words, making them dance in circles. Morality is both an effect and a cause, both an illness and a remedy. There is nothing fixed about our moral values, nothing that is good or bad in itself. The difficulty is to trace the historical movement that led to the formation of our values. Those who view the "good" as something of objective value ignore the historical origin of the concept: "*the slave revolt in morality*: that revolt which has a history of two thousand years behind it and which we no longer see because—it has been victorious" (I, §7).

The story is situated at the prehistory of mankind. It begins with a relatively simple set of assumptions that gradually become more complex and consequential. Nietzsche relates a struggle between the masters and the slaves on the meaning of the good life. The masters are physically strong and able, and they enjoy satisfying their desires without regard to the good of others. The world is theirs for the taking. The slaves, by contrast, learn to deny their immediate instincts. They must devise an alternative view of the world wherein selflessness is a virtue. Satisfaction is still the motivating cause, only for slaves it is achieved indirectly by denying their wants.

Let us look more closely at the details of the *story* Nietzsche tells. To begin with, we should remember that it is a story, and its characters represent philosophical notions rather than historical truths. While Nietzsche claims that the idea of goodness as nobility is in fact historically prior to the idea of goodness as selflessness, nothing much hinges on the historical truth of his claim. The point is not to replace one truth with another but to recast our very conception of how meanings and particularly values become truths.

Obviously this history tells a story about the origins of morality, but it is also about the relations between desire and knowledge, which makes *philo-sophia*. The main characters are the noble warrior—usually a bronzed blond man, who devours whatever he comes across and shows no weakness—and the slave, a weak plebeian, usually Jewish, who abstains from action, represses his desire, and retreats into himself. The highest, ruling caste first referred to itself as noble, good, beautiful, and truthful. The others, in contrast, were bad, common, weak, and miserable. Nietzsche argues that at first these words were bound to political realities, and only later did they achieve the more symbolic form, designating superiority or inferiority of soul. How did it happen that the political contrast between good and bad, which distinguished the high from the low, turned into the moral difference between good and evil? It was the Jews who initiated this abstraction, and in so doing they reversed the value judgments (which Nietzsche, like all good Jews, is now reversing back again):

> It was the Jews who, with awe-inspiring consistency, dared to invert the aristocratic value equation (good = noble = powerful = beautiful = happy = beloved of God) and to hang on to this inversion with their teeth, the teeth of the most abysmal hatred (the hatred of impotence), saying "the wretched

alone are the good; the poor, impotent, lowly alone are the good; the suffering, deprived, sick, ugly alone are pious, alone are blessed by God, blessedness is for them alone—and you, the powerful and noble, are on the contrary the evil, the cruel, the lustful, the insatiable, the godless, to all eternity; and you shall be in all eternity the unblessed, accursed, and damned!" . . . that with the Jews there begins *the slave revolt in morality*: that revolt which has a history of two thousand years behind it and which we no longer see because it—has been victorious.

(I, 7)

This might sound like a piece of Nazi propaganda, a variation on the anti-Semitic forgery "The Protocols of the Elders of Zion," and it was indeed used for such purposes. But Nietzsche bluntly and conspicuously voices views that had persisted ever since the Jews were blamed for murdering the son of God. He expresses these ideas so coarsely and vigorously that they end up sounding a bit ridiculous.

In order to motivate change one needs to begin where one is—with one's prejudices. This is true both in cases of individual therapy and on a grander, collective scale. Nietzsche saw himself as a "cultural physician," and his first order of business was to diagnose the malady, which enables him to proceed by experimenting with treatments. We should remember that the text, as its subtitle suggests, is an exercise in "polemics." He does not intend us to accept it at face value. Instead, the argument should provoke us and ignite a reaction. Nietzsche uses the force of argument to awaken us from our dogmatic slumber.

How then did the Jews, which Nietzsche presents as weak, resentful people of common, slavish descent, manage to pull this off? And are they not the stronger if they are able to transform the values of the old aristocracy? As a first clue, Nietzsche, the "lover of words," indicates that he who commands language commands the world. Nietzsche himself is ~~nothing~~ but a spinner of words, and this is a text, after all. ,wHg chms

Nietzsche offers several linguistic clues for answering this question. He refers to *ressentiment,* a word that resembles the English *resentment* (I, §10). But in French the root lacks a connotation of hatred. *Sentiment* takes on the prefix *re,* which designates repetition or return. *Ressentiment* is essentially reactive. It defines the movement of the desire of the slave, his particular sort of denial of instincts. The slave's emotional energy is unable to discharge itself outside. Because of weakness or fear, he cannot simply act on what he desires. When this satisfaction is denied, the direction of emotions is reversed. Desire bitterly returns to itself and creates an imaginary realm in which it can be compensated. *Ressentiment* is desire forced back onto itself, and this return of the repressed creates the inner space of consciousness. This inner realm is essentially fictional since it serves as an alternative to activity in the real world. But it is a fiction that will transform the reality of the human world.

The power of *ressentiment* is the power of the slave, because only the slave encounters resistances that force him to direct his desire back onto himself. We can also phrase this reactivity in its temporal context: the slave cannot enter into a direct conflict with the master, so his desire is always suspended and confined within him as a potential. Because this emotional energy cannot remain inactive, it therefore carves out an imaginary, virtual world where it can remain alive. The slave avenges himself by creating a fictitious "other world" in which his desires are fulfilled, and he is rewarded for his restraint. So he stores the evil deeds of the master in memory to envision punishments in the other world. The language of virtual reality is entirely appropriate, since the world of the slave is, at first, no more than an alternative to the real world. The master, on the other hand, discharges himself immediately of his impulses. He has no need of consciousness or memory and requires no elaborate formulae to compensate himself in imagined worlds (I, §10).

The story about the master and the slave is therefore also a story about knowing and about desire, or, more accurately, it is about desire turning into knowledge or desire reflected back onto itself creating an inner space where it is preserved in the form of knowledge, ideas, or values. Consciousness and cunning, the ability to store in memory and to keep scores is the slave's contributions to humanity, in Nietzsche's conception. To him these traits are both a sign of illness and an achievement. The slave morality is a symptom of the inability to act concretely or immediately. But it is a remedy *palliative* since it creates an alternative domain to exercise the will. While the master is bound to his physical existence, the slave creates a new realm of activity that is imaginary but no less significant. The creation of subjectivity—that inner fictional space—is the creation of the slave (I, 13). Finally, with the revolt of the slaves, which is imaginary before it is real, the human animal became interesting and deep (I, 6). Now a human being exists both in the real and in the imaginary; it can be strong in one register and weak in the other. Now there is consciousness and there is thinking. Now we can play with the signifiers and decide where our values lie. Now we shape our world. It is a story, after all, and the Jews are indeed the people of the book.

Vertigo—Losing Ground

The Genealogy shatters rigid institutions that, like morality, present themselves as having an objective existence that is inflexible and impervious to change. It enables us to return to the state in which we were the determining and creating force. Historical forces, Nietzsche claims, are important not in understanding the true nature of things, but in appreciating the impossibility of such a thing as a true nature. Nietzsche presents genealogical investigation as a contrast to the stagnation inherent to fixed ideas, dogmatic convictions, and all other "brain sicknesses." For the genealogist, "a tremendous new prospect opens up . . . a new possibility comes over him like a vertigo, every kind of mistrust, suspicion, fear leaps up, his belief in morality, in all morality, falters" (preface, §6). Genealogical inquiry liberates "fixed ideas" by offering quasi-historical stories about the development of convictions and beliefs. The result is that, inevitably, these values become questionable, contingent, partial, or fragile, that is, they are made tangible and flexible.

The genealogist, as Michel Foucault writes in his essay about Nietzsche, "finds that there is 'something altogether different' behind things: not a timeless and essential secret, but the secret that they have no essence or that their essence was fabricated in a piecemeal fashion from alien forms."[5] This vision is as liberating as it is terrifying. Through the twists and turns of the plot, we suddenly recognize ourselves as the communal authors of this narrative, and regaining our agency is a way of making us responsible. Acceptance of this ownership and responsibility is necessary for acting as moral agents. So the play that reveals morality as "just a play" is morally enabling, whereas the play that hides its constructed character is immoral. Thus Nietzsche claims that rigid, ahistorical morality is actually immoral because it makes us passive and dead to our own lives and the lives of others. Morality, as tradition has it, denies our rules as creative agents. It teaches us to reject our desires or rather to turn our desire against itself. Finally, it teaches us to desire not to desire; it teaches us nihilism.

Philosophy and Nihilism

It is worth noting that the charge of nihilism was directed against all the philosophers we have discussed so far. Socrates was accused of subverting the state's established order, introducing new deities, and corrupting the souls of the young. Spinoza was banned from the Jewish community of Amersterdam and his name was equated to heresy. Rousseau was banished from Geneva and France for espousing radical new values of individual freedom that challenged the authority of church and state. Nietzsche himself flirts with nihilism. He too sees life as at bottom meaningless. But for him this means that we are free to create our meanings rather than fall into despair. Life does not come ready-made with value. That's what all nihilists discover. But the philosopher embraces this condition as a source of freedom while the ascetic priest rejects this life and this world for the sake of salvation after death.

Ascetic ideals include obstinacy, self-control, self-mastery, and, importantly, self-creation. The word comes from the Greek *askein,* which means "to work" in the sense of being a practitioner (*asketikos, askts*), later a practitioner of religious devotion—a hermit or a monk. As Pierre Hadot, the eminent French classical philosopher, explains, asceticism was first developed as an exercise of body and mind required by sportsmen and philosophers alike. Socrates embraces this practice in controlling his lustful desire and reshaping it into the desire for knowledge. So the problem is to distinguish methods that seem similar but end in radically different results: on the one hand, the philosophical ability to shape her world, and, on the other, the religious denial of this world for the sake of another.

The philosopher and the ascetic priest show a number of similarities in Nietzsche's *Genealogy*; in fact, it seems that the latter evolved from the former, just as Christianity evolved from Jewish morality, which itself originated from the slave revolt. At a certain stage of human development, the ascetic priest was a true therapist. He helped his suffering congregation deal with "deep depression, the leaden exhaustion, the black melancholy of the physiologically inhibited" (III, 17). The priest alleviated suffering not by curing the disease but by inventing a cause for the pain. It was an ingenious technique since there is no greater suffering than suffering in vain. And the priest was able to save his parishioners by asserting that they had caused their own suffering: "'I suffer: someone must be to blame for it'—thus thinks every sickly sheep. But his shepherd, the ascetic priest, tells him: 'Quite so, my sheep! Someone must be to blame for it—*you alone are to blame for yourself!*'—This is brazen and false enough: but one thing at least is achieved by it, the direction of *ressentiment* is *altered*" (III, 15).

Why is the philosophical method better than that of the priest? The answer cannot be that the philosopher is telling the truth whereas the priest's interpretation is false. Perspectivism means that interpretations have no deeper reality or truth. So we have to rephrase our question: why is the philosopher's *story* better than the priest's? The answer must be that it is more viable and open to differences: it allows for a greater variety of interpretations and it is open to shifting circumstances and to historical transformations. It is, in a word, perspectival. The philosopher does not claim that one universal method can care for the self. His therapy is essentially open, whereas the priest offers his cure as the one and only truth. The priest ignores historic development, perspectives, and differences in context. He treats all pain as essentially the same and prescribes one universal vision of the good life: "The ascetic ideal has a *goal*—this goal is so universal that all the other interests of human existence seem, when compared with it, petty and narrow; it interprets epochs, nations, and men inexorably with a view to this one goal; it permits no other interpretation, no other goal; it rejects, denies, affirms, and sanctions solely from the point of view of *its* interpretation" (III, 23). The belief in truth as something divine—independent, transcendent, or utterly nonperspectival—is the highest value of all religious faiths. Curiously, Nietzsche adds that rigid belief in truth will ultimately spell religion's own death: the uncompromising faith that "God is truth, that truth is divine" brought about the demise of religion and the rise of dogmatic faith in science (III, 24). After all, faith in an omnipotent entity does not withstand the measures of truthfulness that religion itself elevates. Science, insofar as it insists on the eternal value of its truths, is nothing but a more refined and abstract variant of the belief in the "other world." It is an even more powerful rejection of the living, historical, and perspectival character of inhabiting the world.

Nihilism comes in many different shape and forms, like a monster that shifts and mutates, and Nietzsche is very adept in following these mutations. Nihilism creeps in whenever the process of creation is forgotten or denied, as when faith denies the perspective it serves. But it is not enough to recognize this pattern in a theoretical way because this knowledge can quickly turn into a new dogma—the dogma that there are no dogmas. We are forever blind to the orienting framework that shapes the truths we live by. Genealogical investigation is therefore not a theory but a practice. It does not offer up additional truths but becomes an exercise of thought and imagination that returns us again and again to our own perspectives.

The *Genealogy of Morals* is then a performance rather than an assertion of perspectivism. The text guides us in how to weave stories, how to make our own narratives and create interpretations that will be viable and compelling enough for us to live by.

Nietzsche presents the third essay of the *Genealogy* as an exercise (*askesis*) in this process—the art of interpretation. It opens with an aphorism taken from Nietzsche's *Thus Spoke Zarathustra*: "Unconcerned, mocking, violent—thus wisdom wants *us*: she is a woman and always loves a warrior" (III, 1). Philosophy is usually translated as the love of knowledge or the love of wisdom, but Nietzsche's aphorism inverts the relationship. It pushes us to ask: if philosophy is the love of wisdom, what does wisdom love? And it answers: wisdom loves ~~the warri~~or—the one who takes it by the hands and put it to work. The essay that follows, so Nietzsche tells us, is an interpretation of this aphorism. But, instead of recounting the love of action in a linear manner, the story starts with the negative claim and details the varieties of nihilism.

It seems to leave this aphorism behind, unattended. And that is precisely the point. The essay will perform rather than interpret how unconcerned and mocking it is of its initial motivation. Or, rather, the interpretation will be this very performance.

Nietzsche's polemical stance in the *Genealogy* reminds us that philosophy is not just a theory but a creative activity. We need to remain free with respect to the material at hand; we need to fight with it or against it while keeping the process under our control. The results will be something to which we ascribe wholeheartedly but don't need to enslave ourselves. It is this ironic stance of commitment to what one knows to be a fiction that saves perspectivism from becoming another form of dogmatism. Perspectivism is not an assertion, not a claim, but a practice—an exercise, a form of joyful asceticism.

Free Spirits and Perspectivism

The free spirits that Nietzsche envisages toward the end of the book are individuals who can live without fixed ideals and without rigid, predefined "meanings" and still maintain an engaged and creative view of the world. Those individuals embrace the partiality of their perspectives and the incompleteness of their knowledge. They aspire to reach a more impartial view not by rejecting their desires but by learning to switch between perspectives. They make room for others because they are constantly in the process of becoming other to themselves. Free spirits learn how to operate without conviction and yet not be paralyzed by hesitation. Their response to the genealogical process is not that "nothing matters." On the contrary, to them everything matters to the highest degree possible because nothing is outside the field of human action. To realize the "truth" of this perspective is to become more sensitive to oneself and more deeply aware and responsible to others.

To ask about the truth of perspectivism is to miss the point. The question itself is misguided; it presupposes the conception of truth that Nietzsche is rejecting. Perspectivism does not mean that all interpretations are equal in value or that we cannot assess the value of different interpretations. On the contrary, the way to judge between interpretations is not by relating them to some independent criterion but by relating them to ourselves—examining the kind of life they shape.

Can we acquire the perspectivist approach and release ourselves from the imperative to know how things are independently of our ways of knowing them? Can we return to the state in which knowledge and love go hand in hand? The book was intended as an exercise; it is not a treatise but a practice. It offers no definitive conclusions but instead demonstrates how to become once again like a child at play, irreverent and unconcerned yet always passionate: the game is quite serious, but it is ours to play.

6

BECOMING OTHER

Foucault's *History of Sexuality*

Michel Foucault, one of the most influential philosophers of the second half of the twentieth century, produced a body of work that offers a dark testimony to the effects of the growing regulation of experience. Much of his work focuses on the power structures—social, cultural, and institutional—that shape and manipulate individual experience. His primary concern is whether and to what extent we can experience differently. His work and his life demonstrate the need to fight for the freedom to think and feel outside the governing social norms.

In his last project, an unfinished trilogy, *The History of Sexuality*, Foucault focused on the shaping and normalizing of the most intimate of human experiences—sexual pleasure. In the clinic and in the hospital, in school and in prison, in course books, magazines, in art and in the media, sexuality is regulated to conform to the dominant culture and its institutions. How we know ourselves as subjects of desire and what we know of ourselves is shaped by external power structures. Foucault used one word to denote this conflation: *power-knowledge* is a matrix that controls and instructs. It molds and manipulates docile bodies. The matrix exists everywhere, and there is no escape. We are not born with a grid for interpreting experiences, there is no "natural way" of making sense of the word, and so these external matrices determine the scope and variety of knowledge and desire. The result is that the Socratic demand to know ourselves proceeds indirectly, as the self gets shaped by culture.

This is a running theme in Foucault's writing. His texts repeatedly elaborate on how power-knowledge relations bring an undefined field of pleasure under circumspection. But his own practice—his own life and texts—provides the evidence of a different kind of knowledge, one that ends not in regulation but in liberation. In his writing Foucault remains pessimistic regarding the possibility of deregulating experience. But his own life suggests the potential to realign knowledge and love rather than fall back into the power-knowledge matrix.

Foucault's reading of the *Symposium* in the *History of Sexuality* gives readers an opportunity to reevaluate desire and pleasure as the roots of philosophy. Socrates, who started this conversation, channeled desire toward the pursuit of truth and power. Foucault reverses the trajectory. His interests lay in making truth and power again serviceable to pleasure.

Life and Death

When he died at age fifty-seven in 1984, Foucault was probably the most famous intellectual in the world. His views concerning the reach of power, limits of knowledge, origins of moral responsibility, and foundation of modern government were hard to grasp—but that didn't stop them from becoming wildly popular. It was not only what Foucault said that was effective, but his very persona, which spoke effectively of the "right to be different."

His death shocked even close followers of his life and work. He collapsed in his Paris apartment in the prime of his career and was rushed to the hospital at Salpêtrière, the very institution he had studied in *Madness and Civilization*. That institution served as a prison for beggars, prostitutes, criminals, and the insane. The coincidence is eerie, since Foucault died from what was then a little-known epidemic—AIDS. Victims of this "modern plague"— like those who suffered from mysterious ailments in previous generations—were seen as outcasts, and the disease was regarded as punishment. In conservative and medical circles, in the media and in the streets, there were outcries to put an end to the lifestyle and sexual practices that supposedly helped the spread of AIDS. When faced with risk, as Foucault noticed years before, a society will develop "a whole set of techniques and institutions for measuring, supervising and correcting the abnormal."[1]

In the weeks before his death, two volumes of his eagerly awaited *History of Sexuality* had appeared. Foucault was then giving lectures in the Collège de France on the "care of the self," as expressed in the cycle of life and death of Socrates. Death was always an interest for Foucault. Already in 1963, in the *Birth of Clinic*, he wrote that to die from the "disease of love" was to experience "the passion." The religious connotations are evident, but Foucault's interpretation was quite the opposite. A death from love gives life a singularity and significance, as the end point of a sentence establishes the meaning of the preceding words. This meaning goes against that of the Christian passion, in which Christ died for the glory of God and was thus made a universal symbol. To die from the passion of man, so Foucault wrote, is to discover the "lyrical core of man, his invisible truth, his visible secret."[2]

The philosopher was thus able to offer a commentary on his death twenty years in advance. As Gilles Deleuze writes, "few men more than Foucault died in a way commensurate with their conception of death."[3] For him, death offered the ultimate "limit" experience—an experience of the limits of experience. His interest—both theoretical and practical—in sadomasochism stems from a similar desire to experience the body's limits and, in the process, discover a new kind of pleasure. Renouncing oneself, giving up one's life completely, for Foucault, was the only way to resist power or thoroughly transform it: "I think that the kind of pleasure I would consider as the real pleasure would be so deep, so intense, so overwhelming that I couldn't survive it. . . . Complete total pleasure . . . for me, it's related to death."[4]

On more than one occasion, Foucault stated that all his work, for better or worse, grew out of his personal fascination with experience. Toward the end of his life his interest shifted to releasing experience from its usual filters, so flirting with risk as a form of transcendence became all the more fascinating. Foucault did not chose his own death, as some have argued, but, like Socrates before him, he did not avoid it either or betray his work to prolong his life. In San Francisco's sadomasochism bars and clubs he discovered a new way of being that was exhilarating both physically and theoretically. Very little of this experience enters the text. *The History of Sexuality* is a dry historical account of the shaping of pleasure to fit the systemic demands of "productive" culture. But combining the text and the life allows for a more nuanced appreciation of Foucault's work. Up until his death Foucault voiced the other demand—to know beyond the limits of oneself and to think and exist differently.

When his body left the hospital, four days after his death, a few friends and admirers gathered in a small courtyard. In a corner Gilles Deleuze, the famous philosopher and a friend, began to read from the preface to *The Use of Pleasure*. From beyond the grave, Foucault's words summarized a life devoted to limit experiences:

> As for what motivated me, it is quite simple. . . . It was curiosity—the only kind of curiosity, in any case, that is worth acting upon with a degree of obstinacy: not the curiosity that seeks to assimilate what it is proper for one to know, but that which enables one to get free of oneself. After all, what would be the value of the passion for knowledge if it resulted only in a certain amount of knowledgeableness and not, in one way or another and to the extent possible, in the knower's straying afield of himself?[5]

With this question mark placed after the known, Foucault returns, as if by a grand sweep, to the tradition of doing philosophy, not as a form of knowledge but as an art of thinking and being differently. Engaging in true philosophy means trying "to know how and to what extent it might be possible to think differently, instead of legitimating what is already known" (*UP*, 8–9). Can we think and experience in new and unregulated ways that defy or overcome power-knowledge structures?

The Dirty Story

The focus of Foucault's *Use of Pleasure* is not just sex and subjectivity but the discourse concerning sex and subjectivity. Foucault is interested not only in the act itself but in our experience and consciousness of sexuality. The two cannot be entirely separated, since our knowledge of sex informs the real practice and real pleasures we experience. Is it not the case today that romantic movies and pornography come to inform our pleasure as poetry and painting did earlier? If one sees oneself having sex as a character in a movie then that way of experiencing it already establishes the dynamics and shape of one's pleasure. The project of *The History of Sexuality* becomes a "genealogy" that analyzes the ways in which people "focus their attention on themselves to decipher, recognize, and acknowledge themselves as subjects of desire" (*UP*, 5).

Contrary to first impression, human sexuality is not only a natural, bodily impulse but also a historical construct. And so, in order to truly explore the subject of sexuality and what it means for human experience, for Foucault, "it was essential first to determine how, for centuries, Western man had been brought to recognize himself as a subject of desire" (*UP*, 5–6).

So let's get down to the dirty business of sex and philosophy, and, indeed, philosophy becomes dirty with Foucault. Foucault seems to enjoy following the ins and outs of desire as it is described and shaped. Foucault loves the little detail, the minute gesture, the smile only you can see, or the aside. He has a way of explaining the rituals, the fine etiquette—the stylization of life—in its intricate and most subtle details. But this is of course related to the very nature of his investigation. It has to do with the construction of an experience in conjunction with the detailed attention given to it in discourse.

His work examines a range of mostly ancient and somewhat obscure thinkers' perspectives on sexuality and considers examples of excess and correct measure. In these works he finds that the dialectics of desire and restraint are two sides of the same coin. Privation is a limitation enforced by the self on itself. Most of the texts he considers probe the theme of desire for the sake of mastery or knowledge. They are conservative and somewhat ridiculous to the modern reader. But Foucault is not interested in criticizing them anachronistically. In fact, he finds them to be engaging the very pleasure they wish to deny or control. Foucault sees his own work as part of this long tradition. He too will probe desire and attempt to articulate it by referencing other texts. And he too will not hinder pleasure but channel and direct it in the only way possible—by producing more text.

Foucault focuses on the ironic fact that treatises attempting to restrict or denounce desire are themselves infused with lust and wanting. This irony is familiar to anyone who has heard an impassioned rant against deviance and sexuality or varieties of sexual behavior. Preachers of austerity do so with the passion and the vigor of an adolescent in heat. The audience, horrified to hear about immoral behavior, eagerly follows its daily dosage of pornography wrapped as crime news or as the latest political scandal. It is clear that the censoring of sexuality is invested with the same passion it denounces or restricts. Foucault relates this to the Greek notion that there can "be no desire without privation, without the want of the thing desired and without a certain amount of suffering mixed in" (*UP*, 43). The *Symposium* embraces the same principle: one desires what one lacks, and the lack is inherent in desire. Philosophy, in Socrates as in Foucault, is an attempt to allocate a positive space for this lack. It is the absence of knowledge—the craving of knowledge that makes its pursuit possible. Likewise, "thou shalt not" as an edict makes desire more pleasurable. Restraint is then the way we structure ourselves as knowing and desiring subjects.

The significance of restraint becomes evident when we place it against the background of our contemporary culture of hedonism. Culture today is not only repressive (even when this repression is itself sexual), one of its defining characteristics is that it teaches us to demand and expect instant gratification at the same time that it makes satisfaction impossible. Hedonism, as it is commonly known, is the belief that life is about having fun. It therefore recommends an excess of pleasure and it places a high value on objects and acts that embrace pleasure at the expense of other values. Hedonism is not necessarily immoral. Hedonism as practiced in the West usually comes with the caveat that one's pleasure should not be at others' expense. "Enjoy life and let the other do the same" is its universal moral command. Foucault, following Socrates and Nietzsche, offers a different schema to the hedonic one where repression is the negation of pleasure. To Foucault, restraint makes pleasure possible, and the balance of pleasure can shape a beautiful existence. Pleasure is given structure by being moderated, and moderation is the way to happiness.

Foucault is definitely not a conservative, but he is also not an unabashed liberal. His focus on sex leads him to the conclusion that continuous, unrestrained pleasure can stifle existence. Sexual liberation is more conservative than first meets the eye. Restrictions can make other pleasures possible. Freud was the first to focus on the fact that restrictions are often sexually invested. And in the first volume of *The History of Sexuality*, in the famous first essay, "We the Victorians," Foucault rejects the common historical telling that, prior to the nineteenth century, Western humanity lived in repression, while modern culture has discovered sexual liberation. According to Foucault, contemporary humanity has lost touch with the pleasures that sexuality once afforded. We think ourselves open and liberal, but our open attitudes—discussions of sex at the dinner table, for example—are simply a call for more probing, more social censoring, more repression. Sexuality today is not open or liberated, but the discourse on sexuality makes it seem so. We talk and talk about sex, but the more talk the less bodily passion prevails. In a sense, sexuality is already its history.

This is Foucault's playful reversal of common assumptions. On the one hand, liberal talk of sexuality is part of the mechanism of repression and, on the other hand, the seemingly repressive limits on sexual behavior are investing sexuality with new and unknown pleasures. Sadomasochism is a good example of how playful subversion can transform restriction back into a form of pleasure. It inserts desire where desire does not belong—forbidden parts of the body, forbidden places or times—and makes it of use again for pleasure.

Unlike "We the Victorians" who fancy ourselves liberals, the Greeks did not find it necessary to define the domain of pleasure as a subject warranting moral evaluation. Their focus was not on jurisdiction but intensity. In this framework every object and every act can be pleasurable when used correctly and in measure, and restraint is the mechanism of that regulation. Greek morality was not directed at the codification of acts or the probation of desire, but rather toward a "stylization of attitudes and an aesthetics of existence" (UP, 92). Before the development of moral codes and ethical evaluations, aesthetics provided the principle for styling and shaping one's life: "a way of life whose moral value did not depend either on one's being in conformity with a code of behavior, or on effort of purification, but on certain formal principles in the use of pleasures" (UP, 89).

In Greek life an individual would not universalize his sexual behavior or actions in a way to be judged by others as appropriate. Rather, he would shape his sexual act in the singular, as an expression of his singular being, so as to give it brilliance "by virtue of the rational and deliberate structure his action manifested" (UP, 62). Being an art, it called for a certain technical ability—a *savoir-faire*—that could shape the pleasure with style, depending on different variables such as need, time, and status.

Sexuality became a matter of ethical deliberation only because it concerned the one most important sector of Greek society—free men. The proliferation of sexual depictions, descriptions, stories, allegories, medical and philosophical treatises, political and social pamphlets, dietary and economic guides show the ways in which desire was first shaped as an "ethical substance." This, for the Greeks, was a task for men—a special art form that took pleasure as its subject: "In the use of male pleasures, one had to be virile with regard to oneself, just as one was masculine in one's social role. In the full meaning of the word, moderation was a man's virtue" (*UP*, 83).

Sexuality for the Greeks was too important and vital to be left unexamined. The way men pursue pleasure is part of a greater "aesthetics of existence"—which is not about the vapid pursuit of pleasure but about freedom and control or the stylization of life according to principles chosen by each individual self.

Originality and Otherness

In the final chapter of what later proved to be his last text, Foucault provides a brilliant reading of the *Symposium*. The *Symposium* is, of course, a story about the love between men, but it's also a story about how humans shape themselves in the presence of another person's desire, how the experience of being desired by another is internalized and how self-experience is changed in the process. It is an intellectual biography of sorts.

Foucault identifies the steps that lead to desire and consummation carefully. First there is the issue of courtship, the detailed attention given to the relations between men and adolescent boys guiding them on how to achieve a beautiful form and so to be aesthetically and morally pleasing. Foucault writes:

> The first was in a position of initiative—he was the suitor—and this gave him rights and obligations; he was expected to show his ardor, and to restrain it; he had gifts to make, services to render; he had functions to exercise with regard to the *eromenos*; and all this entitled him to expect a just reward. The other partner, the one who was loved and courted, had to be careful not to yield too easily. . . . Now, this courtship practice alone shows very well that the sexual relation between man and boy did not "go without saying": it had to be accompanied by conventions, rules of conduct, ways of going about it, by a whole game of delays and obstacles designed to put off the moment of closure and to integrate it into a series of subsidiary activities and relations. In other words, while this type if relation was fully accepted, it was not a matter of indifference.

(UP, 197)

The relationships between men are significant to the Greeks not because they deviate from nature or are reproductively unproductive. Such conceptions are products of our own "sexually liberated" culture. Instead, it was the Greeks' high esteem for such relationships between men that made them the subject of scrutiny. In the ancient Greek world, male homosexual relations were the only form of sexuality practiced by free individuals. In heterosexual relations, sexual pleasure was problematic because of statutory conventions enabling the husband to govern his wife, estate, and household. Inherently, sexual relations raised questions of rights and responsibilities. But in the case of the relation between men, "the ethics of pleasures would have to bring into play—across age differences—subtle strategies that would make allowance for the other's freedom, his ability to refuse, and his required consent" (UP, 199).

For the Greeks, the ethics of pleasure was most pressing for the boy entering a sexual relation with an adult man. The boy, a future free and governing member of society, was to submit to the desire of the other. But this submission must make room and prepare for his future autonomy. Later, in Europe, adolescent girls and women would face the same problem of guiding feelings, desires, rules of courtship, and beauty to navigate between granting and withholding desire. In Greece boys played the same game of temptation and resistance in situations fraught with inner paradoxes. Foucault refers to this somewhat ironically as the "antinomy of the boy":

> On the one hand young men were recognized as objects of pleasure—even the only honorable and legitimate objects among the possible male partners of men. . . . But on the other hand, the boy, whose youth must be training for manhood, could not and must not identify with that role. . . . In short, to delight in and be a subject of pleasure with a boy did not cause a problem for the Greeks; but to be an object of pleasure and to acknowledge oneself as such constituted a major difficulty for the boy. The relationship that he was expected to establish with himself in order to become a free man, master of himself and capable of prevailing over others, was at variance with a form of relationship in which he would be an object of pleasure for another. This noncoincidence was ethically necessary.

(UP, 221)

Foucault reads the *Symposium* as an attempt to provide a solution to this paradox. How can relations between men and boys become honorable and preserve desire, while allowing room for the other's freedom? Socrates' speech as well as Plato's depiction of the events that transpire between the participants are attempts to solve this paradox—the paradox of how to transform the object of pleasure into a subject in control of his pleasure.

The relations between love and knowledge become very evident on this reading. Socrates is interested in making desire self-conscious so that it can take hold and shape itself. His speech shows the way in which desire achieves self-knowledge. The Socratic solution consists, according to Foucault's reading, in replacing the problematic of courtship and honor with that of truth and restraint (*UP*, 231). When Socrates gives his speech, the issue is no longer the question of maintaining a boy's honor or determining who to love under what conditions that allow lover and beloved to keep their virility. These questions are subordinated to another more fundamental question: what is love in its very being, what is true love? This is no longer a question of etiquette, of conduct and pursuit, but an ontology of love—a search for its essence. For modern readers, accustomed to the idea that love has an essence or that there is a truth in love, such a transformation might pass in silence. We no longer appreciate the radical nature of connecting the discourse of love with that of truth. But such a conception was wholly alien to the participants of the *Symposium*. Love had to be presented as a (semi) divine intervention in what seemed like a natural concern with how to win over someone else and keep both parties' honor.

Against the common reading of the *Symposium*, Foucault positions the body at the center of the discourse as the place where the lines of pleasure and truth intersect. Socrates' love is sustained only when he is able to resist physical love and to the extent that he is able to master his temptation. This does not mean that he does not love or desire, but rather that the force of true love causes him to postpone the consummation of his desire indefinitely. This resistance, drawn from the body, becomes the source of a new and yet unknown pleasure. Postponement allows him to channel love and desire into wisdom. It is now the master's wisdom and not the boy's honor that is the mark of true love, and it is this that attracts the loved one and keeps him from "yielding": "Socrates introduces another type of domination: that which is exercised by the master of truth and for which he is qualified by the dominion he exercises over himself" (*UP*, 242).

The curious thing is that homosexual desire is exalted at the same instant that it is excluded. Such desire is pure, and, as such, it transcends the flesh and becomes part of the perfection of the idea. Socrates introduces a method for elevating desire, separating it from the love of fleeting physical beauty, to the love of beauty itself, which is eternal and universal. Thus desire is directed toward truth, which for Socrates is the very name for what is eternal and universal. It is curious since this dynamic is lost in the development of Western discourse on sexuality. We are left with the restriction without the higher pleasure these regulations once afforded.

In this game of truth, desire encounters its own nature; it knows itself to be formed around a lack. It is not the physical object that satisfies it but the perfection that it can achieve when it resists being tempted by physical satisfaction. The lack of object satisfaction is what desire is, in truth, the lack that it revolves around and guards. It is the source of animation—desire's very life. The Socratic innovation is to turn desire around absence rather than toward an object. This is an ingenious solution because it serves pleasure while channeling it to truth. But realizing this premise outside the Greek context would involve a full rejection of pleasure in the name of abstract, disembodied truth. Hence the one form of relation, which was deemed most important and pleasurable because it was free, will be denied in the future in the name of what is "proper," "right," "in essence," "by God's will," or "in nature." According to Foucault, this misreading overlooked the original Platonic intention and context, but it transformed our forms of experience. The meaning of the body, its pleasures, vices, moderations, and limits will never be the same.

Socrates' speech on love reveals the possibility of a blissful state in which pleasure and wisdom coexist. It is an Edenic vision, suggesting a return to existence before eating the fruit of knowledge. In this state the body serves as a vehicle of knowledge, sex is a discovery of knowledge and pleasure, and reproduction is not necessary because eternal life is granted. The Edenic state is therefore both wholly sexual and pure. We, in our fallen state, get glimpses of such embodied knowledge in moments of bliss or orgasm. We reunite as one, but only for a fleeting moment. In this vanishing moment we recognize what we have missed—the possibility of an embodied, naked communion, both carnal and transcendent. Socrates' speech captures this moment wherein love is knowledge and knowledge is bliss. But at the very moment they achieve unity they are also split. The pleasure that Socrates wanted to elevate and preserve soon dies. In knowledge sexuality will be denied, and in love there will be no knowledge. Sex will be allowed as means of reproduction, rather than a vehicle of pleasure and wisdom. As if the punishment for eating the forbidden fruit still applies in the split between the body and the mind. And if pleasure is allowed, it will only be dumb pleasure without voice and without content.

With his rereading of the *Symposium,* Foucault achieves a double purpose: on the one hand, he shows that the history of sexuality underscores the formation of modern subjectivity. Our own history is narrated back to us in such a way that we come to know ourselves as products of a long, involved historical battle. We become characters in a play, shaped by texts and the interpretation of texts, taught how to experience and modeled as desiring subjects. But, at the same time, this very text shows the construction to be just that, a construction, one among possible alternatives. By revealing the process of shaping experience, it shows us the extent to which experience can be unmade and made otherwise. Understanding sexuality as a history is itself liberating. We are reminded that sexual experience is part of a narrative created over time that can change even in our lifetimes. This understanding allows us to regain our agency as desiring subjects, and the text itself provides a guide for how free individuals can shape their desire and give meaning to pleasure.

But beyond this history of desire, beyond the making and remaking of pleasure, beyond the subject of desire, there arises a radical question concerning the possibility of living outside the matrix of power-knowledge. Can there be a pleasure that is not suffused in hierarchy and power, knowledge and mastery? Foucault seems to suggest that the power-knowledge matrix is necessary for pleasure. His reversal of the Socratic trajectory, leading knowledge back to pleasure, is convincing. But it is just one more example of the ways in which knowledge and power are fused. Following Foucault's narrative, we do not escape the knowledge-power matrix; we simply retell the story. And so we are left with the question whether there could be something like raw, unstructured, and unregulated experience. Can we think, bring into discourse, and realize an experience of radical openness? Can we experience knowledge in love and love in knowledge?

Maybe such an experience today can only appear under the guise of death. And, indeed, for Foucault the release became possible only as the shattering of the self in pleasure. At the end only death provided a release from social norms and taboos. Why did he leave his passion outside the text? Why did he not let other pleasures be brought into discourse? And can we do otherwise? Can we give voice to pleasure and make it a form of wisdom without yielding to accepted norms? Can power be transformed again, not by power but by love? And is love then the knowledge that power cannot recognize?

7

DERRIDA'S "HERE I AM"

Jacques Derrida was my teacher in New York before his death from cancer in 2004. As a lecturer, he was formal, careful, and generally lacking in any overwhelming personal charm. Most of the time, he would read his notes for a book he was completing, as if the paper shielded him from his students or from his own mistrust of himself as a teacher. But witnessing the subtlety of his thought was a marvel. His lectures attempted to create new ways of using language. He tried to strike a balance between comprehension and disorientation by sharing his texts in a foreign tongue before a mostly American audience. He did not presume the authority of a teacher or performer, but we appreciated his honesty, which itself became a new source of authority. His teaching enacted the Socratic method by adapting it to our times: a person debating himself, inserting doubt between thought and words. There was nothing like it. We would leave the lecture without fully understanding the experience but nevertheless transformed.

His notes, which he examined with the scrutiny of a harsh reviewer, were always about the text of another philosopher. He acknowledged that this practice was parasitic, feeding on the thoughts of others and using them to light his own spark. But, in so doing, the texts he read would come to life again and develop meaning beyond their original contexts. In Derrida's reading texts became battlegrounds for interplay between the explicit meaning of a text and other emergent meanings that were contained but not strictly controlled in its language. This is deconstruction in a nutshell—a way of reading and writing that does not assert new knowledge but triggers understandings encapsulated in other texts. Deconstruction, as the term suggests, both creates and destroys the authority of the text by exposing its generative framework. In this way it brings to light a literary unconscious—an unacknowledged undercurrent that flows through a text and that animates its language.

Nonidentity

Derrida lived a life of nuanced distance from his own biography, not unlike Iago's claim in Shakespeare's *Othello*: "I am not what I am." He never hid his roots as a Jewish Algerian who immigrated early to France, but did not explicitly identify with that life story either. His life was marked by what he called *différance* spelled with an *a* rather than an *e*, to signify the act of becoming other than oneself, an act that is usually imperceptible but leaves its mark. Like the intentional "mistake" in the French spelling, the shift can only be read but not heard.

Born in 1930 in El Biar, then part of French Algeria, Derrida was the third of five children and was named Jackie after Jackie Coogan, a Hollywood child actor best known as Chaplin's sidekick in *The Kid* (1921). He changes his name later to Jacques to fit his adopted Parisian environment. On his first day of the high school year, in 1942, Derrida was expelled by administrators implementing anti-Semitic quotas imposed by the Vichy government. He chose not to attend the Jewish school and explained later that he did not identify with the other displaced students and teachers who formed it. There is nothing particularly intellectual in his background: he wanted to become a soccer player and twice failed the entry exam to the École Normale Supérieur before finally being admitted in 1951. His philosophic career became part of the important developments of post–World War II France, as he became friends with Louis Althusser, later a well-known Marxist critic, and took classes taught by Michel Foucault with whom he was first a friend and later a rival.

His own philosophical voice emerged with three groundbreaking books, all published in 1967: *Writing and Difference, Speech and Phenomena,* and *Of Grammatology.* In these works Derrida introduced his unique method of close-reading texts and emphasized the power of language to unsettle their "official" philosophical claims. His criticism centers on the semblance of authority and the pretense of coherence inherent in most philosophical texts. He applied Iago's assertion, "I am not what I am," directly to the texts he examined. Through close readings of the movement of a text, Derrida shows how texts mean different things at once, at times, inadvertently, contradicting themselves. This is what Derrida terms *différance*, a neologism playing on the fact that, in the French, *différance* can signify both differ and defer. The full meaning of a word or a text can never be gathered in one instant, but is always the result of a play of differences with other words and other texts, a play that extends over the structure of language and shifts when read in different contexts at different times. This internal *différance* is not accidental; in fact, Derrida shows again and again, difference is essential for the meaning of the text.

Call this the essential law of impurity: nothing is simply what it is, because it is also its other. This law cannot be stated because it is self-contradictory. How can you make a law that claims to deny the identity of things without denying the very law itself? This echoes other paradoxes we have covered: knowing you don't know, communicating solitude, and deregulating experience. But it seems closest to the paradox of perspectivism in Nietzsche. If all meaning is a perspective, what do we do about the claim of perspectivism itself? Derrida learned that lesson well: he will not state the law of impurity (that's my fault), but would rather show its work and put it to work repeatedly. He will expose the textual unknown—what the text represses or excludes, disowns or refutes—and show that this very exclusion is necessary for the text's own identity.

His early writings set the tone and establish the deconstructive method that will be the hallmark of Derrida's work. Deconstruction is not a theory but an operation—a way of writing that establishes itself by disrupting other texts. In this manner it creates a tradition from a series of seizures, a tradition of impossibilities, if not an impossible tradition.

Cinematic Biography

Derrida was an intellectual celebrity, documented in films, on TV, and on the Internet. With him, for the first time in years, philosophy again acquired a "star" and spokesperson in mainstream culture. His mother's inspiration came true as Jackie's life became the stuff of documentary. As he did in all public appearances, Derrida mastered the performative dimension of philosophy: the process of portraying himself involved playing someone else and acknowledging this artifice.

A documentary from 2002, titled *Derrida*, tries to unravel Derrida's tangled philosophical legacy by beginning with the question of the "future."[1] Derrida distinguishes between two senses of the word: the first is the common, temporal designation and the second involves an ethical and existential openness to risk or the unexpected—"what is to come." The French word, *avenir*, indeed includes what is to come, *a-venir*, which Derrida translates as "the as-of-yet unreal," "the unexpected," "unthinkable," "to-come." Deconstruction is known as an attack on ideas that present themselves as perfect or complete and fully contain themselves in the here and now. Such notions of identity and purity come at the cost of excluding other meanings and preventing transformation. Raising the question of the future, the movie refutes any ideology of purity. It makes room for the improper that does not belong. Like Derrida's deconstruction, it welcomes the parasite or the other.

When Derrida is asked to explain deconstruction, he shifts and seems uncomfortable with the contrived nature of the scene:

> Before responding to this question, I want to make a preliminary remark on the completely artificial character of this situation. I don't know who is going to be watching this, but I want to underline, rather than efface our surrounding technical conditions, and not feign a "naturality," which doesn't exist. I've already started in a way to respond to your question about deconstruction, because one of the gestures of deconstruction is not to naturalize what isn't natural—to not assume that what is conditioned by history, institutions, or society is natural.

After voicing his frustration with the artificiality of the interview, he quickly transforms his mood and the room's setting into part of his response to the question. His reaction becomes a self-conscious performance of the essence of deconstruction. He refuses to "feign a 'naturality.'" But how can he reject an on-camera interview as artificial without raising the same concerns about other media in which his philosophical message is disseminated? Aren't those constraints involved in text as well? Why does it seem to follow that thinking with a camera is more or less natural than with a pen?

As he explains in the film, deconstruction involves calling attention to the unseen sets, hidden lighting, and obscured microphones that makes appearances look impeccable. By exposing the process involved in creating the scene, the inevitability or naturalness of the final product is chipped away, and we can see not only the infrastructure that holds it together but the choices and contingencies that lead to the end result. Deconstruction appeals to those who have a taste for raw creation rather than those who prefer to see only a glossy final product. To do deconstruction, as Derrida writes in *Memories for Paul de Man*, and the movie quotes, is to do "memory work."[2]

The idea that deconstruction, or philosophy in general, generates no new knowledge is not unfamiliar for us. Socrates pioneered this argument in claiming he knew nothing and had nothing to tell. Plato developed a variation on this idea when he created his theory of reminiscence, in which learning is remembering what we once knew but subsequently forgot. Spinoza insisted that the whole exists from the very beginning. Rousseau added the recommendation to do nothing and let thought go its own way, and Nietzsche and Foucault looked backward into the history of our concepts and practices in order to reengage the present. Derrida updates this insight by insisting that returning to the origins of a text is sufficient to transform it. In the text we shall soon examine, Derrida reads the work of his teacher and in so doing reshapes both the original message and his own original contribution to the future of philosophy.

When the filmmaker, a former student of Derrida, asks him to talk about love, Derrida is visibly annoyed. How can he speak about "love?" It is too general, he claims. So he introduces a distinction between the "who" and the "what" of love. According to Derrida, the "what" involves a set of characteristics we identify as appealing in our beloved. The "who" is a unique singularity that always eludes us. Derrida adds that when we love someone we usually feel unable to explain why; we love the individual because of the singular person that she or he is. When we fall out of love, we often attempt to produce specific reasons, but they are always incompatible with what drew us to love in the first place. This discrepancy shows the difference between the idea and the reality of love. Love is always torn between knowledge and mystery, and yet the two must coexist to appreciate the unique singularity of another person.

At this point the viewer inevitably comes up with the most common criticism of Derrida, also voiced by his readers—that he intentionally misleads us and uses difficult language to cover the simplicity of his ideas. I tend to agree with this criticism. His work is intended to make us come to terms with the obscure nature of our linguistic acts. What we take for granted is determined only by repetition and normalization. There is nothing natural or neutral in our common and cherished interpretations. In the film this intentional ambiguity comes off as a personality trait, which it surely is. But in his writing confusion becomes a part of the philosophy—one that joins hands with the tradition, seeks to return to the guiding questions, and undermines our intellectual and normative foundations.

In the film, Derrida often seems as brusque and off-putting as Socrates. He does not come from a pedigree of intellectuals, nor does he seek to embody the sense of celebrity implicit in being the star of his eponymous film. Instead, he stands alone in the kitchen, spreading butter on bread or watching TV, as he discusses philosophy. He resists the effect of "celebrity," which is inherent to moviemaking. He will remain ordinary, holding onto his secret, like everyone else.

To Derrida, like Socrates, this very ordinariness is an essential part of philosophy because the discipline is an approach to life, rather than a religion or exercise in idol worship. To be just ordinary is perhaps the most open and radical gesture. Just. Ordinary. His ideas are simple; in fact he has nothing to say. There is no special gift philosophy requires other than the commitment to think and to live a life that is open to reflection. As in love, our guide or partner can be anybody, but, at the same time, the philosopher is as unique and inimitable as any other.

Obligation

Toward the later part of his life, Derrida was concerned with death and with philosophy as a "preparation for death." His work from that time involves experiments with the forms of memoir and eulogies dedicated to the many friends and colleagues he lost during those years. He focuses on ethical-political considerations of forgiveness, responsibility to the dead, terror, and the death sentence. This chapter follows the eulogy he delivered on the occasion of the death of his philosophical muse—the French Jewish philosopher, Emmanuel Levinas—later published in *Adieu à Emmanuel Lévinas* and as part of the English collection *Psyche: Invention of the Other*.[3] It is by all means a difficult text, both in content and in form. It reveals Derrida's way of reading in its fully developed stage. Taking issue with his own philosophical background, Derrida commemorates and explores Levinas's moral philosophy. For us, it is the proper ending for a book that begins with Socrates' death and continues with the final or posthumous writings of Spinoza, Rousseau, Nietzsche, and Foucault.

Our text opens with an epilogue that reads like a torn fragment:

At This Very Moment In This Work Here I Am

—He will have obligated[4]

At this very instant, you hear me, I have just said it/ He will have obligated. If you hear me, already you are sensitive to the strange event. You have not been visited, but just as after the passage of some singular visitor, you are no longer familiar with the places, those very places where nonetheless the little sentence—where does it come from? Who pronounced it?—lets its resonance still wander.

Clearly, this text begins in the middle of a conversation, and we as readers immediately have the sense that we have missed something. It addresses us directly, "you hear me," and yet the words seem not to speak to us or provide answers. He asserts "here I am" and that we can hear him, but how? How can he be "here" when, as readers, we absorb the text alone? How can we hear him? This striking opening passage relies on the power of language to distract us from the literal progression of words and to carry us through a set of associations. This path leads to dimensions of meaning that remain unspoken but are nevertheless present whenever communication takes place. Encountering this text for the first time might leave us with the sense that we are being manipulated by wordplay or obfuscation. But, by disorienting us, Derrida creates room for us to relate to a text not only by means of understanding but also through personal experience. This method of reading asserts that understanding—at least the conscious work of figuring out the author's intentions—is only one part of the process, and perhaps not the most important one.

This initial confusion reawakens us to the realization that philosophy, like any other discourse, is often locked inside the conventions of everyday communication and may be domesticated like any other animal. It gradually loses its surprising, piercing voice and, in the process, sacrifices its ability to jostle us from the everyday. Because Derrida's language is still strange and nontransparent, it allows us to experience how we make sense rather than retreat to conventions. Derrida's text ravishes meaning with selfreferential wordplay, the effect of which is to reveal the operation of language and make us aware of its artificiality.

Since this text is also an act of commemoration, it asks what debt we owe to our forbears and mentors. How can we pay tribute to them? How do we preserve them or let them speak from within our text? And, more particularly, in what way is Levinas present in Derrida's text? In what way are all my teachers present when I write, here and now, in the present? What kind of obligation do we carry to those who sparked our thinking? And how can we repay our debt?

It was Levinas who taught Derrida that responsibility is the primary structure of subjectivity. According to Levinas, any ability to respond to the other (response-ability) structures me as a subject. The other calls on me before I know who I am, and my response to this call will define what I will become. This premise reverses the usual moral intuition, according to which I can only be responsible for what I can control. The notion that only a self-governing subject can be morally responsible for her actions is based on the belief that subjects are and can be autonomous. Levinas does not begin there, but rather with the other. I am responsible for you, because without you I am not even a self. Ethics for Levinas is grounded in such relations and not in the self-sufficient subject. It even precedes me as a person: my actions and responses to the other make me the person that I am, rather the other way around. Responsibility is the very foundation of philosophy since it comes before being and before knowledge.

The notion of the other has been with us from the outset of our philosophical interrogation. Socrates begins with the other, since he has nothing to say, and his desire to know—the origin of *philosophia*—is rooted in his being fractured and incomplete. Spinoza rejects the idea of an autonomous will, Rousseau takes himself as another, and so does Nietzsche, who begins by asserting that "we are necessarily strangers to ourselves." Foucault calls upon us to become other than ourselves. Derrida begins his focus on the "other" by referencing an unseen character:

—He will have obligated ["Il aura obligé"].

As the text progresses, each section reinterprets this epigraph. This technique, in which Derrida opens with a disorienting claim and constantly reexamines this claim throughout the text, conjures up Nietzsche's cryptic beginning to his third essay of the *Genealogy*:

—Unconcerned, mocking, violent—thus wisdom wants us: she is a woman and always loves only the warrior.

So we have our plate full. We have a feast. It is overwhelming at times: too much is going on at once, too many thoughts, too many references, and too many meanings and voices piled together without a clear hierarchy or organization. Again, my problem here is to make this philosophical excess clear, passing on to you the effect of reading such a text, and stressing that the confusion is necessary. But on the other hand, my task is to show you a way in, keep you interested, making you understand it bit by bit. Can one understand without ceasing to feel confused? Can the understanding focus on this very confusion without necessarily overcoming it?[5]

Let's apply this logic to the epigraph itself, which initially seems so confusing that it verges on being meaningless: "He will have obligated." The questions cascade from this opening: Who is obligating whom? When? Why? And in what way? The obligation is not associated with a person and conveys no specific burden. If it doesn't place demands on anyone in particular—either to execute or receive—then how is the obligation effective in any way? How can it "work" at all? Or perhaps, alternatively, this lack of specificity makes it effective in another way because it obligates everyone?

The temporal structure of the epigraph provides revealing clues as to its meaning. It is made in the future perfect, which makes it simultaneously future and present. On the one hand, it foresees the future and, on the other, it conveys an obligation on an unnamed subject in the present. This structure gives it a haunting presence—it hovers over everyone indefinitely because it is addressed to no one at any particular moment.

We can also think of it as a promise seen from its end point, as if already fulfilled. In the future, you will have fulfilled the obligation. For instance, I can promise you that if you finish this chapter, you will have completed 134 number of pages. This pledge projects us into the future. I promise you something by making you imagine what will happen if my promise is satisfied. My promise is like a contract, an obligation. Your finishing the book guarantees that you will have read 134 pages. You might not finish, but if you do, that reality is guaranteed. I promise you.

But if the claim is a performative one, then it must be a special case, since a performative is always voiced in the present by a singular person. At this moment I promise, I commit myself in some way, and I take on an obligation. A performative is a way of doing something in language. It is an activity, rather than a description of fact. It constitutes the reality that it describes. Action always takes place in the present. But the epigraph creates a hypothetical form of obligation, as an inverted promise made by an unspecified "he." In Derrida's words, it is "a performative without present" (*IO*, 173). It is an activity whose enactment has not yet taken place, a working without a work, a happening that makes nothing happen. A performative without a present event has something of the biblical voice—the voice of creation or even the language of creation in the Bible. Derrida will quote from the Songs of Songs and will name his mentor, Emanuel Levinas, in acronym *EL,* which is "God" in Hebrew and "she" in the French homonym.

In the original Hebrew the biblical voice combines past and future, exactly like "he will have obligated," though this use of tense is lost in subsequent translations. Instead of "and God has spoken," the Hebrew literally reads: "and God will have spoken" (ויאמר). Instead of "and God called onto Abraham," it literally reads: "and God will have called onto Abraham" (ויקרא). Again, the future perfect tense creates a cascade of questions: Did it happen already, is it happening now, or will it happen in the future? Of course, the answer to these questions affects our reading and our beliefs. If we don't know what is said, what do we believe? Or perhaps belief is at stake only when we don't know for certain? The events never actually happen in a grounded, concrete manner; instead they continue to hover, eternal and suspended, as possibility.

Derrida comments on his usage of this tense later in the essay. He suggests that, though the future anterior (also called the future perfect) is a disorienting tense, he has no alternative but to use it. The same constraint binds anyone who wishes to comment on the reading of the text but is not present to have the dialogue in real time. The use of this tense implicates all of us through an obligation. It connects us as family, and we can address each other or avoid one another because there is always already an implicit obligation weaving us together.

This seemingly convoluted construction is actually a feature of our everyday communication. Whenever I address you, when a question is asked, when someone comments, when a dialogue proceeds, when a diary is written, and even when thinking takes place in language without an outward expression, an obligation arises through this communication, even if it is not addressed to a particular audience. First of all, it is the obligation to make sense, to understand, to be clear, or to make an effort. In short, it is the obligation to communicate, which must be assumed even when the complexity of reading or writing overwhelms us.

The floating temporality of the obligation is simply another feature of linguistic communication, even of "the least virtuoso writing," as Derrida argues (IO, 173). This performance is everywhere, always, already. Derrida's "Here I am" makes explicit that every text is an act of communication. It is even more apparent because the communication here is so difficult. It is impossible since Derrida is not here, nor am I. But yet you hear him through me. As Derrida continues: "But you aren't uneasy, what you feel is something unheard-of, yet so very ancient—it's not a malaise, and even if something is affecting you without having touched you, still you have been deprived of nothing" (*IO*, 143). This reassurance is also an instruction: if we let the text do its work, even if we don't understand it in full, it will act on us, read us, and perhaps even transform us. We will be affected without having been touched. Two impossibilities (now and at no time) that cannot meet because they are on the two extreme ends of temporality, meet nevertheless, and, at this moment, the text becomes an event.

Giving

What I remember most from Derrida is the immense attention, his almost ritual-like devotion to the text. Sometimes for an entire semester, a single quote—or even a single word—would hang in the air. This stage allowed the special charisma of Derrida to come to the fore, even though he would barely raise his eyes from his notes. In his lectures philosophy returned to its poetic sources—to the times when it expressed itself in fragment or parable and moved listeners through use of creative words. Aristotle deviated from this tradition by writing like a university professor. These writings were canonized in medieval thinking, which made his style seem mandatory for any "serious" thinking. We are only now, gradually and slowly, relaxing from the clutch of this Western tradition. Many are surprised that philosophy can be more than a set of arguments aimed at creating definitions and building theories. In its original form, philosophy is also an open invitation to thought, reading, or practice. And switching our paradigm—thinking of philosophy as a form of poetry or art—relieves the anxiety of nonunderstanding and opens us to the possibility of being affected by words without fully mastering their meanings. A text works in many ways. Understanding it is just one way of being affected and reacting to it or participating in creating its meaning is another.

Derrida's text wants to extend its arms and touch us, and we might want to receive its teaching, but temporal impossibility stands in the way. The author's "I" and the reader's "me" can never actually coexist: "I won't pronounce your name nor inscribe it, but you are not anonymous at the moment when here I am telling you this, sending it to you like a letter, giving it to you to hear or to read, giving it to you being infinitely more important to me than what it might transmit at the moment" (*IO*, 146). The act of giving is more important—"infinitely more," according to Derrida—than what is given in communication. What is at stake then is neither understanding nor knowledge, modeled on the traditional sense of possession and mastery, but transmission itself. Derrida writes that he cannot repay his debt to Levinas. The gift he has received is not any specific item or piece of knowledge, but rather the act of passing, transmitting, and giving itself. His debt to Levinas can only be repaid by passing on a similar gift. This text therefore pays tribute to his teacher by making us his students too. If we are touched by those words then we too are obligated. If the words communicated something it all, he will have obligated.

Receiving a gift creates an obligation, and that is part of the difficulty inherent in Derrida's text: "Nothing is more difficult than to accept a gift. Now what I 'want' to 'do' here is to accept the gift, to affirm and *reaffirm* it as what I have received" (*IO*, 147). Nothing is more difficult then to accept the gift—this is why people respond to gifts with "you shouldn't have." Nothing is more difficult because a true gift—one that merits the name—cannot be returned and instead creates a cycle of obligation. And how do you pass on thinking: not the thought, not the knowledge you gained, but the act itself? Derrida wants to pass along this gift in the text, which in turn obligates us, as his readers, to become custodians of the gift and to accept what neither he nor we can possess. Now the question turns to us: how are we to respond to this text? Derrida explains the cycle: "And if it is thus that (in my turn) I give to you, it will no longer form a chain of restitutions, but another gift, the gift of the other. The invention of the other" (*IO*, 147–48). Our reading becomes more than an interpretation—it is an acceptance of obligation: "Your reading is thus no longer a simple reading that deciphers the sense of what is already found in the text; it has a limitless (ethical) initiative" (*IO*, 161). Derrida writes that we are coauthors of his text. But this act of writing on our part is also not in our control. We participate in the writing of the text, and that text is about little other than the writing of texts. A philosophical text does nothing if it does not allow for an exchange of thoughts. The reader can only respond, for example, here and now by passing it on.

Love

silence

According to Derrida, there must be something in communication or in relationships that defies quantification or calculation. Thinking and communicating create a movement that cannot be regulated or controlled and, when transmitted to another person, cannot be returned. Love is another name for what we give without regard for what we receive in return. And giving the gift of love to others, making them lovers able to love others and not just our loved ones, is perhaps the greatest gift we can bestow.

The very act of giving—extending oneself, letting go—is not dependent on a reciprocal return. It is an exchange of sorts, but one that goes beyond a zero sum economic game. This openness to whatever comes, Derrida admits, is strange:

Suppose then: beyond all restitution . . . I desire . . . to give to EL. This or that? Such and such a thing? A discourse, a thought, a writing? No, that would once more give rise to exchange, commerce, economic, reappropriation. No, to give him the very giving of giving, a giving that would no longer even be an object or a present said. . . . This "giving" must neither be a thing nor an act, it must somehow be someone. . . . Strange, isn't it, this excess that overflows language at every instant and yet requires it, sets in incessantly into motion at the very moment of traversing it?

(*IO*, 148)

This cycle of language inscribes us in an ongoing process of transmission. We are woven into the chain that extends from the immemorial past, preserved in texts, to the future existence of new texts, and so on. We, as readers and future writers, are the necessary emissaries. But at each moment, we must be more than ourselves. That is our peculiar position in Derrida's address to Levinas. Derrida repeatedly uses the first- and second-person singular (*I* and *you*) to make himself present to the reader. But both "I" and "you" are as indeterminate as they are singular and unrepeatable. They represent whatever singularity is to emerge out of the reading. It could be anyone's reading and anyone's writing. But it also must be you and me.

The voices are blurring—ours, the voice of the text through an "I" that is everyone and a "you" that is anybody. Derrida quotes Levinas on love and says it is a sickness or a psychosis that shatters individual boundaries and simultaneously makes you and me possible. In love we lose ourselves, but without love we are not fully individuated: "the identity of the subject is here brought out, not by resting upon itself, but by restlessness that drives me outside of the nucleus of substantiality" (*IO*, 151).

In reading Plato's *Symposium* we found that desire is produced by a lack or absence, and this lack defines desire, because one inevitably seeks what one lacks. Derrida, following Levinas, reverses this logic. For both, desire is compared to an overflow or an act of generosity. I desire insofar as I'm *too much* for myself, always beyond myself, flowing over to the other. This might at first seem counterintuitive, but it works well with Levinas's and Derrida's notion that I am not complete without opening myself to the unexpected and uncontrolled presence of the other. We need to bestow our love on others; we need to give even before we can receive. Toward the end of the text, he quotes the Song of Songs, that eternal song of love that David supposedly dedicated to the creator: "I opened to my beloved; / but my beloved had gone away. He had disappeared. / I was outside myself when he spoke to me. . . . I called him and he did not reply . . . / I implore you, daughters of Jerusalem / If you find my beloved, / What will you say to him? . . . / That I am sick with love" (*IO*, 153). Love means to open oneself and accept the unknown. In love being contaminated with otherness becomes a formative experience. Derrida explains it most eloquently by invoking Levinas and writing about his mentor's ability to create a text composed of interruptions: "Nearly always with him, this is how he fabricates the fabric of his work, interrupting the weave of our language and then weaving together the interruptions themselves, another language comes to disturb the first one. It doesn't inhabit it, but haunts it. Another text, the text of the other, without ever appearing in its original language, arrives in silence" (*IO*, 152–53). That might have well been said about the present text. Derrida creates new interruptions and weaves them together to form a new text, which jostles its predecessor, Levinas's work. But it does not subsume Levinas; instead, the two share a haunting coexistence.

In this way the philosophical corpus is a series of structured interruptions that overflows beyond itself from the beginning. It needs us, the readers, to make its claims communicable. We do that not merely by "understanding" or "knowing" but by reproducing its effects and leaving new legacies. The Socratic unknowingness must be revived with every new generation, in every text. Like a torch whose light travels silently from hand to hand and mind to mind, it is a labor of love.

NOTES

1. UNDOING KNOWLEDGE

1. Plato, *The Dialogues of Plato*, trans. R. E. Allen (New Haven: Yale University Press, 1984), vol. 1, Stephanos 17a–18a. Hereafter, all quotes use the Stephanos system of pagination found in most modern editions of Plato.

2. Gregory Vlastos, *Socratic Studies* (Cambridge: Cambridge University Press, 1994), p. 4.

3. For a detailed account, see Jonathan Lear's *Open Minded* (Cambridge: Harvard University Press, 1998), p. 162.

4. Sigmund Freud, "Three Essays on the Theory of Sexuality," in James Strachey, ed., *Standard Edition of the Complete Psychological Works of Sigmund Freud* (London: Hogarth, 1953) 7:134. Hereafter SE followed by volume and page number.

5. Otto Apelt, *Platonische Aufsätze* (Leipzig: Teubner, 1912), pp. 96–108.

6. Søren Kierkegaard, *The Concept of Irony*, ed. and trans. H. V. Hong and E. H. Hong (Princeton: Princeton University Press, 1989), p. 214.

2. THE LOGIC OF DESIRE

1. Pierre Hadot, *Philosophy as a Way of Life* (Oxford: Blackwell, 1995), p. 158.

2. Sigmund Freud, "Group Psychology and the Analysis of the Ego," *SE* 18:91.

3. Sigmund Freud, "Resistance to Psychoanalysis," *SE* 19:218.

4. Plato, *Symposium*, trans. A. Nehamas and P. Woodruff (Indianapolis: Hackett, 1989), Steph. 191D.

5. Jacques Lacan, *The Four Fundamental Concepts of Psychoanalysis,* ed. Jacques-Alain Miller, trans. Alan Sheridan (New York: Norton, 1981), p. 235.

6. Jonathan Lear, *Open Minded* (Cambridge: Harvard University Press, 1998), p. 150.

7. See Nehamas's introduction to the *Symposium*, p. xxv.

3. UNDER A CERTAIN FORM OF ETERNITY

1. Benedict Spinoza, *Ethics*, trans. E. Curley (London: Penguin, 1996), V, P67. I follow the traditional reference system for the *Ethics*—beginning with the part in Roman letters, D for definitions or P for propositions followed by their number, and C or S for the corollary or the scholium.

2. Stuart Hampshire, *Spinoza and Spinozism* (Oxford: Clarendon, 2005), p. vii.

3. Gilles Deleuze, "Spinoza and Us," in *Spinoza: Practical Philosophy* (San Francisco: City Lights, 1988), p. 122.

4. In a famous letter to Max Born, a leading proponent of an indeterminist interpretation of quantum theory, Einstein wrote, "you believe in a God who plays dice, and I in complete law and order in a world which objectively exists"; *The Born-Einstein Letters*, 1916–1955: Friendship, Politics and Physics in Uncertain Times, trans. Irene Born (New York: Walker, 1971), December 4, 1926. Interestingly, Einstein also confessed his belief in Spinoza's utterly rational and necessary God: "I believe in Spinoza's

God, Who reveals Himself in the lawful harmony of the world, not in a God Who concerns Himself with the fate and the doings of mankind"; P. A. Schilpp, ed., *Albert Einstein: Philosopher-Scientist* (Chicago: Open Court, 1970), pp. 659–660.

4. COMMUNICATING SOLITUDE

1. Jean Jacques Rousseau, *Reveries of the Solitary Walker*, trans. Peter France (New York, Penguin, 1979), p. 27; hereafter *Reveries,* followed by the page number.
2. Quoted in Maurice Cranston, *The Solitary Self* (Chicago: University of Chicago Press, 1997), p. 5.
3. See, for example, Eli Friedlander, *J. J. Rousseau: An Afterlife of Words* (Cambridge: Harvard University Press, 2004), p. 11; hereafter *An Afterlife of Words*.
4. René Descartes, *Meditations on First Philosophy*, ed. John Cottingham (Cambridge: Cambridge University Press, 1996), Second Meditation, 25; hereafter, Second Meditation.
5. Ludwig Wittgenstein, *Tractatus Logico-Philosophicus*, trans. D. F. Pears and B. F. McGuinness (New York: Routledge, 1992), 6.4311.
6. Rainer Maria Rilke, *Rilke on Love and Other Difficulties*, trans. John J. L. Mood (New York: Norton, 1975), pp. 27–28.

5. HOW WE BECOME WHAT WE ARE

1. Friedrich Nietzsche, *On the Genealogy of Morals*, trans. Walter Kaufmann (New York: Vintage, 1989), preface, §1. Hereafter all quotes are followed by part and section number.
2. See Walter Kaufmann's introduction to *On the Genealogy of Morals* in the *Basic Writings of Nietzsche* (New York: Modern Library, 2000), p. 447.
3. Alexander Nehamas, *Life as Literature* (Cambridge: Harvard University Press, 1995), pp. 1–4.

4. Friedrich Nietzsche, *Will to Power*, ed. and trans. Walter Kaufmann (New York: Vintage, 1968), § 452.

5. Michel Foucault, "Nietzsche, Genealogy, History," in *Language, Counter-Memory, Practice*, ed. Donald F. Bouchard, trans. Donald F. Bouchard, Sherry Simon (Ithaca: Cornell University Press, 1977), p. 142.

6. BECOMING OTHER

1. Michel Foucault, *Discipline and Punish*, trans. Alan M. Sheridan-Smith (New York: Vintage, 1995), p. 198.

2. Michel Foucault, *The Birth of the Clinic*, trans. Alan M. Sheridan-Smith (New York: Vintage, 1994), p. 174.

3. Gilles Deleuze, *Foucault*, ed. and trans. Seán Hand (Minneapolis: University of Minnesota Press, 1986), p. 95.

4. Michel Foucault, "The Minimalist Self," in Lawrence D. Kritzman, ed., *Politics, Philosophy, Culture* (New York: Routledge, 1988), p. 12.

5. Michel Foucault, *The History of Sexuality,* vol. 2: *The Use of Pleasure*, trans. Robert Hurley (New York: Vintage, 1990), pp. 8–9; hereafter *UP*.

7. DERRIDA'S "HERE I AM"

1. *Derrida*, directed by Kirby Dick and Amy Ziering Kofman (Jan Doe Films, 2002).

2. Jacques Derrida, *Memories for Paul de Man* (New York: Columbia University Press, 1986).

3. Jacques Derrida, *Psyche: Invention of the Other*, ed. Peggy Kamuf and Elizabeth G. Rottenberg (Stanford: Stanford University Press, 2007); hereafter *IO*.

4. Derrida's translator also offers the original French of Derrida's text: "Il aura obligé."

5. Friedrich Nietzsche, *On the Genealogy of Morals*, trans. Walter Kaufmann (New York: Vintage, 1989).

INDEX

Islam Enlght ⎧ Brwn   54   edit
   Bellaigue   ⎨ Baake   78   x = 1-y
              ⎪ Adarand   98   outline
              ⎩   ↘ matrix